Malaysia and the "Original People"

THE CULTURAL SURVIVAL STUDIES IN ETHNICITY AND CHANGE

Allyn & Bacon

Series Editors, David Maybury-Lewis and Theodore MacDonald, Jr.
Cultural Survival Inc., Harvard University

Indigenous Peoples, Ethnic Groups, and the State, by David Maybury-Lewis

Malaysia and the "Original People": A Case Study of the Impact of Development on Indigenous Peoples, by Robert Knox Dentan et al.

Forest Dwellers, Forest Protectors: Indigenous Models for International Development, by Richard Reed

Malaysia and the "Original People"

A Case Study of the Impact of Development on Indigenous Peoples

Robert Knox Dentan
State University of New York, Buffalo

Kirk Endicott
Dartmouth College

Alberto G. Gomes
Latrobe University

M. B. Hooker
formerly of the University of Singapore

Allyn and Bacon
Boston • London • Toronto • Sydney • Tokyo • Singapore

Vice President, Social Science: Sean W. Wakely
Series Editor: Sylvia Shepard
Series Editorial Assistant: Erika Stuart
Marketing Manager: Karon Bowers
Cover Designer: Jenny Hart
Electronic Composition: Siobhan Curran

ISBN: 0-205-19817-1

Printed in the United States of America

10 9 8 7 6 5 4 3 2 1   01 00 99 98 97 96

Contents

v

Foreword to the Series

Cultural Survival is an organization founded in 1972 to defend the human rights of indigenous peoples, who are those, like the Indians of the Americas, who have been dominated and marginalized by peoples different from themselves. Since the states that claim jurisdiction over indigenous peoples consider them aliens and inferiors, they are among the world's most underprivileged minorities, facing a constant threat of physical extermination and cultural annihilation. This is no small matter, for indigenous peoples make up approximately five percent of the world's population. Most of them wish to become successful ethnic minorities, meaning that they be permitted to maintain their own traditions even though they are out of the mainstream in the countries where they live. Indigenous peoples hope therefore for multi-ethnic states that will tolerate diversity in their midst. In this their cause is the cause of ethnic minorities worldwide and is one of the major issues of our times, for the vast majority of states in the world are multi-ethnic. The question is whether states are able to recognize and live peaceably with ethnic differences, or whether they will treat them as an endless source of conflict.

Cultural Survival works to promote multi-ethnic solutions to otherwise conflictive situations. It sponsors research, advocacy and publications which examine situations of ethnic conflict, especially (but not exclusively) as they affect indigenous peoples, and suggests solutions for them. It also provides technical and legal assistance to indigenous peoples and organizations.

This series of monographs entitled "The Cultural Survival Series on Ethnicity and Change" is published in collaboration with Allyn and Bacon (the Simon and Schuster Education Group). It will focus on problems of ethnicity in the modern world and how they affect the interrelations between indigenous peoples, ethnic groups and the state.

The studies will focus on the situations of ethnic minorities and of indigenous peoples, who are a special kind of ethnic minority, as they try to defend their rights, their resources and their ways of life within modern states. Some of the volumes in the series will deal with general themes, such as ethnic conflict, indigenous rights, socio-economic development or multiculturalism. These volumes will contain brief case studies to illustrate their general arguments. Meanwhile the series as a whole plans to publish a larger number of books that deal in depth with specific cases. It is our conviction that good case studies are essential for a better understanding of issues that arouse such passion in the world today and this series will provide them. Its emphasis nevertheless will be on relating the particular to the general in the comparative contexts of national or international affairs.

The books in the series will be short, averaging 100 to 150 pages in length, and written in a clear and accessible style aimed at students and the general reader. They are intended to clarify issues that are often obscure or misunderstood and that are not treated succinctly elsewhere. It is our hope therefore that they will also prove useful as reference works for scholars and policy makers.

David Maybury-Lewis
Theodore MacDonald
Cultural Survival, Inc.
46 Brattle Street
Cambridge, Massachusetts 02138
(617) 441-5400 fax: (617) 441-5417

Preface

"THIS BOOK TOLD ME MORE ABOUT PENGUINS THAN I WANTED TO KNOW"

Our main goal is to show, by means of a concrete case study, how development and government programs in a developing country can affect indigenous peoples. Readers interested in the general problems of tribal peoples in the modern world may feel that we provide too much detail about specifically Malaysian phenomena and not enough general analysis. Like the school child whose apocryphal book report we quote as the title to this section, they may feel that this book tells them more about Malaysia and Orang Asli—the aboriginal peoples of Peninsular Malaysia—than they want to know. But social scientists base their abstract concepts on analyses of the lives of real people in real places at specific times. Different people examining the complicated social phenomena we describe may draw different abstractions from them. A comparison with other sets of equally complex social phenomena from other places or times can indicate whether the abstractions have general applicability. Only after immersion in particular cases can students hope to make valid generalizations about "the dynamics of development" or "the plight of native peoples."

Anthropologists claim that students of development, in their rush to generalize, often conflate phenomena which are fundamentally dissimilar and mutually incommensurable. A statistic like "acres under cultivation" may include swiddens (temporary fields) and irrigated fields; orchards and gardens;

rice, rubber, gardenias, cranberries, alfalfa, and even (in Malaysia) butterflies. Numbers are extremely important in making comparisons, but, as the philosopher Bertrand Russell once remarked, numbers are also a way of giving the same name to two or more things which are not alike. It is important that, in counting or comparison, we make sure that the phenomena we count or compare are alike along some meaningful (abstracted) dimension. To know that, we need familiarity with the raw data.

Moreover, as ethnographers, we agree with linguists that meaning comes from context. "High infant mortality" means something different to someone who has never seen a dead baby than to someone who has helped other mourners carry a little corpse to its grave. The "dynamics of development" and "the plight of native peoples" are empty shibboleths for anyone who does not get down and dirty with the empirical facts in all their frustrating detail.

Our other objective in this book is to make Orang Asli and their current situation known to the world outside a narrow circle of academic specialists. We hope that once fair-minded people—in Malaysia and elsewhere—know about Orang Asli and their problems, they will want to help them. Like indigenous minorities everywhere, Orang Asli get little attention in the international press. Only when there is an "incident," such as the blockading of logging roads by Penan people in Malaysian Borneo, does the media pay attention. Once the incident is over, the people—and their problems—fade back into obscurity.

Even the Malaysian general public knows little about Orang Asli. The average town- or city-dweller may never have seen an Orang Asli, or, having seen one, may not have recognized him for what he was. Malaysian schools teach next to nothing about them. Coverage of Orang Asli in the local press is haphazard and often ill-informed. Those articles that do appear usually reflect the government's views and wishes for them. A common genre of articles describes a politician pontificating (usually just before an election) about what the government is going to do for a certain group of Orang Asli; there is seldom a report afterward of whether it actually happened.

Although the Malaysian government rarely coerces the media directly, it controls them in numerous ways (see, e.g., Karp 1994). The government runs television and radio, and political parties in the ruling coalition own substantial interests in all major national newspapers. Any magazine or newspaper published for general circulation must obtain permits from the government each year. In 1991, the Prime Minister denied permits to the newspapers published by opposition parties, thus reducing them to "newsletters," which could only circulate to registered party members. In 1987 the government made an example of *The Star*, then the second largest English-language daily (over 150,000 circulation), closing it for five months and forcing an editorial reorganization. Many of its best reporters fled to Hong Kong. The Internal Security Act (ISA), enacted by the British colonial government during the Communist insurgency in the 1950s and in force ever since, allows for arrest without warrant of people accused of "subversion." The police can hold them for sixty days without charge or review, and the Minister of Home Affairs can extend their detention indefinitely without trial (Human Rights Watch and Natural Resources Defense Council 1992:55-6). Under the ISA the government can seize whole press runs of local or foreign publications. It did so when *Asiaweek*, a Hong Kong-based newsmagazine, covered the "Srigala incident" in which government agents bulldozed an Orang Asli-built church (Chan Looi Tat 1991; see Chapter 3). Finally, other restrictions on press freedom include an Official Secrets Act modeled on Britain's and a set of constitutional amendments which forbid discussing the privileges granted Islam and Malays (Human Rights Watch and Natural Resources Defense Council 1992:53-54). The press is thus technically "free" in that it censors itself, either because one of the owners is a government party or because the editor worries about getting his annual permit. Even foreign publications distributed in Southeast Asia censor themselves to avoid government sanctions (Ramsey 1994).

Although Malaysian newspapers and magazines never challenge government policies toward Orang Asli, they occasionally report instances in which particular programs are failing. This is helpful, as it sometimes leads to the responsible agencies rectifying the problems. For example, in February 1985 the *Malay Mail* published a front-page article on the squalid conditions at an Orang Asli school hostel (Manavalan 1985a). Among other problems, 280 children were living in quarters meant to house 80. The school's administrators had repeatedly appealed to the Department of Aboriginal Affairs (*Jabatan Hal Ehwal Orang Asli*; abbreviated JHEOA) and the Education Department for aid, but to no avail. Within a few months of the article's publication, however, the authorities had made numerous improvements and even promised to landscape the school grounds to create a "garden atmosphere." Service clubs and private individuals had also donated needed equipment (Manavalan 1985b, 1985c). But such reports are few and far between. The public has no way of knowing about the many similar or even worse problems for Orang Asli that persist beyond the gaze of the media or which the media are too timid to report. It is heartening, however, that a recent poll conducted by the *New Sunday Times* showed that 88 percent of respondents wanted to know more about Orang Asli (*New Sunday Times* 1995).

Besides their ignorance of Orang Asli, much of what Malaysians think they *do* know about Orang Asli is wrong. In that same poll, 82 percent incorrectly answered that most Orang Asli live in reserves, and 14 percent thought they lived in trees! Most Malaysians' ideas about Orang Asli are inaccurate—often derogatory—stereotypes. Even government officials hold and perpetrate such stereotypes. For example, JHEOA officers often claim their programs are intended to get Orang Asli to give up their "nomadic" lifestyle. Nomadism has highly negative connotations in the Malay world view, as we will show. But in fact less than 5 percent of Orang Asli have even a tradition of frequent residential movement. The vast majority are farmers of one type or another whose ancestors were basically sedentary for hundreds or even thousands of years. Unfortunately, not only the views of ordinary Malaysians but also the bulk of government policies toward Orang Asli rest on such misconceptions. We hope this book will help Malaysians correct this situation.

We will present some of what we have learned about Orang Asli life, describe the conditions in which Orang Asli now find themselves, and share our understanding of how those conditions affect them. We also try to convey the ideas and wishes of Orang Asli themselves, paying particular attention to statements by emerging educated Orang Asli intellectuals and leaders. But we also present what we have heard from ordinary Orang Asli villagers, whose voices seldom reach outside their communities and whose views bureaucrats usually dismiss. During our extended periods of living with Orang Asli, they have shared with us many hopes and fears and questions about the future. By mingling our lives with theirs we have inevitably absorbed their point of view on the events now affecting them. If that is a bias, it is a bias that sorely needs to be expressed. Theirs is the voice least heard in discussions and debates over the Orang Asli's future.

Obviously the people most qualified to provide accurate information on Orang Asli cultures and Orang Asli points of view are Orang Asli themselves. Ideally they would have written this book. But, for reasons we will discuss, the number of Orang Asli with advanced education in social sciences remains tiny. The first Orang Asli anthropologist, Juli Edo, is still working toward his Ph.D. at The Australian National University. Until the time comes when Orang Asli academics can speak loudly for themselves, we offer this book as an interim step.

The authors bring different viewpoints and expertise to the project. What we share is our extended intimate contact with Orang Asli and concern for their welfare. Robert K. Dentan (Ph.D. Yale, 1965) is Professor of Anthropology and American Studies at the State University of New York at Buffalo. He lived with Semai in Pahang and Perak states from late 1961 to mid 1963, with Perak Semai for a year between mid 1991 and mid 1992, and made brief visits to them in 1975 and 1993. In 1976 he spent six months with Btsisi' (officially called "Mah Meri") on Carey Island off the Selangor Coast.[1] He also stays in touch with Orang Asli by mail. He has studied such varied topics as Orang Asli knowledge of the rain-

---

1. Dentan thanks The Ford Foundation for a Foreign Area Fellowship Training Grant in 1961-1963, The Guggenheim Foundation for support in 1991-1992, and the American Museum of Natural History on both occasions.

forest flora and fauna, social relations, conceptions of dreams, and relations with other ethnic groups. His publications include *The Semai: A Nonviolent People of Malaya* (Holt, Rinehart and Winston, 1968/1973). Kirk Endicott (Ph.D. Harvard, 1974; D.Phil. Oxford 1976) is Professor of Anthropology at Dartmouth College. He lived with Batek in Kelantan for a total of almost two years, during four field trips between 1971 and 1990.[2] His research concentrates on their economy, social organization, and religion. He has published articles on various aspects of Batek culture and on the effects of development on Orang Asli in general. His publications include *Batek Negrito Religion* (Clarendon Press, 1979). Alberto Gomes (Ph.D. The Australian National University, 1986) is Senior Lecturer at La Trobe University. Born and educated in Malaysia, he is now an Australian citizen. He has done extensive research on economic, social, and demographic change among Jahai in Kelantan (1976-1979, 1988), Temuan in Selangor (1978), and Semai in Perak (1982-1984 and 1986-1988).[3] He has published numerous articles, chapters, and reports and has co-edited two books, including *Modernity and Identity: Asian Illustrations* (La Trobe University Press, 1994). M. B. Hooker (LL.M. University of Canterbury, 1965), now retired and living in Australia, was formerly Lecturer in Law at the University of Singapore and Professor of Comparative Law at the University of Kent at Canterbury. He lived with and studied Semai in Perak at various times between 1966 and 1969 and in later visits in 1973 and 1980.[4] He has a special interest in the legal status of Orang Asli. His publications in-

2. Endicott's research was supported by grants from the National Institute of Mental Health, the University of Malaya, The Australian National University, the Social Science Research Council, the U.S. Department of Education, the Claire Garber Goodman Fund, and Dartmouth College. He thanks all these agencies.
3. Gomes gratefully acknowledges financial support from the University of Malaya and The Australian National University.
4. Hooker thanks the Ford Foundation and the University of Kent at Canterbury, U.K. for supporting his research.

clude *Adat Laws in Modern Malaya* (Oxford University Press, 1972) and *The Personal Laws of Malaysia* (Oxford University Press, 1976).

ACKNOWLEDGMENTS

The authors wish to thank the Orang Asli friends who have graciously taken us into their lives over the years and shared their knowledge with us. We also thank all the friends and colleagues in Malaysia who have kept us apprised of events involving Orang Asli. We are grateful to the Malaysian government for giving us permission to do research in Malaysia and to the Department of Aboriginal Affairs (JHEOA) for permission and assistance in carrying it out.

Some of what we say in this book is critical of the government and the JHEOA. Criticism may seem a rotten way to repay the support they gave us in the past. We only hope our remarks will be taken in the spirit intended—as constructive criticism. We try to provide a factual foundation upon which more effective policies can rest. The non-Malaysian authors do not claim that the policies of our own countries toward indigenous minorities are superior to Malaysia's. We simply wish to help Malaysia avoid reproducing the mistakes that our countries have already made.

We dedicate this book to all Orang Asli. All royalties will go to their benefit.

Introduction

ADVANCING RAPIDLY TO WEALTH AND GREATNESS

> *The colony of a civilized nation which takes possession either of a waste country, or of one so thinly inhabited, that the natives easily give place to new settlers, advances more rapidly to wealth and greatness than any other human society.*
>
> Adam Smith, *An Inquiry into the Nature and Causes of the Wealth of Nations*

> *We stay poor and everyone else gets rich. The Chinese get rich. The Indians get rich. The Malays get rich. And they all get rich from the land of us indigenous people. Is that fair?*
>
> Bah Tungkoont, *Semai man*

Visitors to Peninsular Malaysia see a dynamic modern society rapidly taking shape in a lush, tropical environment. Peninsular Malaysia (also called "West Malaysia" and "Malaya") is the part of the Southeast Asian nation of Malaysia located on the Malay Peninsula, a tongue of land about the size of New York State that extends southeastward from the southern border of Thailand to the island city-state of Singapore. Malaysia also includes two large states, Sarawak and Sabah, on the island of Borneo. In the north the Malay Peninsula is

1

divided lengthwise by a range of mountains which flattens out in the south. Rivers flowing out of the mountains have formed broad alluvial plains along both sides of the Peninsula. Being just north of the equator, the Peninsula's climate is hot and wet. Dense, towering cumulus clouds produce sudden downpours that often sweep across the land in the afternoon, briefly transforming streets into streams. The daily showers merge into continuous rain during the southwest monsoon, from June to September, and the northeast monsoon, from November to February, when rivers may swell and burst out of their banks. The natural vegetation of the Peninsula is tropical rainforest, ranging from alpine forest on the mountain tops to mangrove forest along the west coast. But the rainforest is giving way more and more to human constructs like plantations, rice paddies, market gardens, tin mines, industrial parks, towns, and cities.

The modern international airport at Subang, fifteen miles outside the national capital of Kuala Lumpur, is surrounded by vast plantations of rubber trees which march in orderly rows over the gently rolling countryside. Going from the airport to Kuala Lumpur, Malaysia's largest city (population 1.3 million), travelers soon enter a multi-laned superhighway connecting the capital with the port city of Klang on the Straits of Malacca. The highway—usually jammed with speeding cars, trucks, vans, and buses—sweeps past an array of modern factories and businesses, many still under construction. It continues through the "bedroom community" of Petaling Jaya, with its tree-lined residential streets, shopping centers, and well-planned industrial parks. On the way to the luxury hotels of central Kuala Lumpur, a visitor's taxi may pass the beautiful Lake Gardens Park, the modern National Museum, and the elegant National Mosque before plunging into the mixture of skyscrapers, government buildings, Chinese shop-houses, and multistoried airconditioned shopping malls that occupy the city center. In 1996 Kuala Lumpur's twin Petronas Towers became the world's tallest buildings. Well-dressed people crowd the sidewalks, shops, offices, restaurants, and open-air markets, men mostly wearing European-style shirts and slacks, Chinese women in fashionable dresses, Indian women in flowing saris, Malay women in

Middle Eastern-style robes with long-sleeved blouses and veils or scarves covering their heads and necks, and children in neat blue and white school uniforms. Government office buildings, parks, shopping districts, and upscale residential neighborhoods dot the hills surrounding the city center.

A few older buildings—the National Art Gallery (once the Majestic Hotel), the Selangor Club, and the ornate "Moorish"-style railway station, law courts, and old central post office—recall Peninsular Malaysia's history as a British colony. Between 1786 and 1918, the British gradually extended their control over the eleven states of Peninsular Malaysia before finally granting them independence in 1957. Many national institutions—such as education, law, and government—reflect British influence. The federal government is a constitutional monarchy with an elected Parliament, an appointed Senate, and a Prime Minister who is the leader of the political party with the most members of Parliament. The states retain a lot of autonomy—having their own Sultans, legislative assemblies, and bureaucracies. Control of land and natural resources resides mainly with individual states. Following a policy of "indirect rule," the British kept the Malay Sultans of the states as nominal rulers. The Malaysian economy also shows colonial influence. The British exploited the Malay states for raw materials, mainly rubber and tin. They built roads, railroads, telephone lines, and post offices to assist in their extraction. The modern economy, like its colonial forebear, mixes capitalist free enterprise with government intervention and control. British entrepreneurs remain among the most numerous foreign investors in Malaysian businesses.

The prosperity evident in Kuala Lumpur—and to a lesser extent in Malaysia's other cities—comes from the country's success in achieving "development" (also called "modernization" or "westernization"), a paramount goal of many "developing" nations. Development is the process by which a country harnesses its natural and human resources to producing wealth rather than merely leaving its citizens to provide for their own needs. Thus it usually means replacing subsistence economies with a market economy. The goal is to generate economic "growth," measured by such indices as Gross Domestic Product (GDP), personal income levels, and consumption rates. Colonial powers usually promote development in their colonies to generate surplus wealth for export back to the "mother country." Most post-colonial governments around the world continued development after independence, but tried to keep the wealth in the country, where it could be used for private investment—like commercial enterprises and housing—or invested in public works—like roads, airports, and government services—which in turn facilitated further development. In their zeal to reach the same level of development as industrialized nations, developing nations often seek capital from external resources, in the form of foreign aid, loans from private banks and international agencies such as the World Bank, and investments by multinational companies.

Malaysia's development has been based on primary industries (production of raw materials); secondary industries (processing materials and manufacturing); and, to a lesser extent, service industries. Despite the occurrence of a depression, recessions, and two World Wars, there has been a general trend toward expansion of primary industries throughout this century, although the mix has been constantly changing due to fluctuations in supplies and demands. Today Malaysia is among the world's leading producers of tin, rubber, palm oil, and tropical timber, and it also produces some petroleum. Tin, a crucial ingredient of bronze, has been obtained from the Peninsula's rich alluvial ore deposits for at least a thousand years. Tin-mining intensified greatly in the nineteenth and twentieth centuries with the introduction of hydraulic mining and dredging. The British started commercial production of natural rubber at the end of the nineteenth century. When the price of rubber fell after World War II, agricultural companies switched to growing oil palm, originally from Africa and now Malaysia's most lucrative plantation crop. In general, Malaysian development planners have favored commercial agriculture to forestry, but logging, the necessary precursor to plantation agriculture, has become a major money-earner in recent years, especially in Sabah and Sarawak. For years, little Malaysia has been the world's major exporter of tropical hardwoods. Oil production, too, is relatively recent, dating from the discovery of oil reserves off the east coast of the Peninsula in the late 1960s. These products are used in local industries, but are even more valued as exports.

Manufacturing industries have flourished mainly since Malaysia's independence in 1957 (colonial powers generally try to prevent their colonies from developing industries that would compete with those of the home country) and especially after the government began the New Economic Policy (NEP) in 1970. The expansion of industrial production has been impressive, reflected in the numerous factories sprouting on the outskirts of the major cities and, except during the global recession of the 1980s, in Malaysia's continually rising gross domestic product (GDP). In the early 1990s, while the President of the United States was blaming an American growth rate of under 2 percent on "a worldwide recession," the Malaysian GDP was rising by about 10 percent per year (*Utusan Konsumer* 1993d).[1] Malaysia is one of the economic success stories of Asia, a favored location for multinational companies seeking to establish factories for labor-intensive industries like electronics assembly and clothing manufacturing.

This growth has been due in large part to government policies encouraging outside investment (Jesudason 1990:166-192). The government has established industrial parks called Free Trade Zones in favored locations and has offered foreign companies inducements such as "tax holidays" (periods without taxation) to encourage them to build factories there. The government has also built up the infrastructure—roads, water supplies, phone service, etc.—for these industrial zones. The biggest attraction to multinational companies, however, is the low wages accepted by Malaysian workers. The government has suppressed the development of trade unions and placed stringent controls on those that do exist.

---

1. The GDP index, however, is somewhat deceptive, since it does not count costs like pollution, overfishing, permanent destruction of rainforest, and so on. How, for example, does one calculate the dollar value of the extinction of "almost all the lowland forests in Peninsular Malaysia"? (Singh 1981:181)

The benefits of Malaysia's economic development have been unevenly distributed. Development is not just economic growth; it is also a process in which wealth and potential wealth shift from some people to others. The winners in Malaysia's development process can easily be seen in the urban areas. Wealthy businessmen are much in evidence, riding in their chauffeur-driven luxury cars between their offices and their lavish mansions surrounded by gardens and high walls. Prosperous professionals and government officials live in luxurious houses and high-rise apartments in the "better" neighborhoods. Expensive and exclusive social clubs serve as the meeting places for powerful politicians and high-ranking bureaucrats, Malay aristocrats, wealthy foreign and local businessmen, and foreign diplomats. Surrounding the cities are sprawling new suburbs of modest but modern and comfortable houses, with small passenger cars (mainly locally-made Protons) in the driveways, housing the rapidly-growing middle class.

The losers in the development process are less visible. They include the mostly South Indian workers on rubber and oil palm plantations whose living conditions and educational opportunities have stagnated since the 1960s. With the fall in the world price for rubber, plantation owners have compensated by raising productivity per worker while holding wages level (Drakakis-Smith 1992:136). Rural peasants, mostly Malays, have also remained near or below the poverty level, as the cost of farming has risen while the prices received for their products, like rice and rubber, have fallen (Drakakis-Smith 1992:81). The picturesque Malaysian villages, so prominent in travel brochures, conceal poverty and an absence of economic opportunities. Workers in old and new industries have also suffered as government and employers have collaborated to keep wages low. Every day large numbers of workers, many of them young women, stream into the industrial estates from nearby villages and towns—by bus, bicycle, motor-bike, and on foot—and take home a meager pay packet at the end of every six-day work week (Ong 1987). As Drakakis-Smith concludes (1992:137), "the limited availability of formal urban employment in general, and of reasonably waged jobs in particular, has already been a factor in the *increase* in urban poverty since 1970" (emphasis in the original).

The people who have lost the most from development in Peninsular Malaysia, however, are Orang Asli, the "original people" or "aborigines." Orang Asli have not only been left behind in the rising prosperity of the nation, their economic condition has deteriorated. They have been transformed from economically independent food and commodity producers to landless wards of the state, confined more and more to dusty regroupment villages where they eke out a living from casual wage-labor, rubber-tapping, and collecting rapidly dwindling supplies of forest produce for sale. This has happened despite the fact that a special government agency concerned with their welfare, the Department of Aboriginal Affairs (JHEOA), has existed since 1954.

The reasons for the decline in the fortunes of the Orang Asli are both obvious and obscure. The obvious reason is that the Orang Asli are a small and politically powerless group of peoples. The land they occupied and the resources they used in their traditional economies are precisely those that more powerful interest groups want for development: forests for logs, rivers for hydroelectric power, and land for plantations, factories, housing estates, airports, and golf courses. Because Malaysian law follows the exploitative British laws and does not recognize Orang Asli ownership of their traditional lands, they receive minimal compensation, if any, for the loss of their land and livelihood. Thus the impoverishment of Orang Asli helps generate the enrichment of bureaucrats, entrepreneurs, and politicians in Malaysian cities. This aspect of their plight is not unique to Malaysia; throughout the world powerful groups appropriate the resources of weak indigenous peoples. The history of the United States is a case in point.

A more subtle reason for the Orang Asli's problems is that the Malaysian goverment's plans for them are full of contradictions and partially hidden agendas which undermine both the programs' effectiveness and also the ability of Orang Asli to adapt to the massive changes around them. The reasons for the flaws in the government's treatment of Orang Asli are specific to the Malaysian situation, but even here there are parallels in the policies and programs for indigenous minorities in other countries.

To detail the reasons for the current plight of Orang Asli and to explain the Orang Asli's reactions to their plight, we must explore not only the cultures of Orang Asli themselves, but also the culture of the Malay ruling class, especially the attitudes and aspirations that shape the government's Orang Asli policies. Development and the subjugation of indigenous minorities are too often portrayed as inevitable processes like forces of nature: "You can't fight progress!" We argue on the contrary that the problems of Orang Asli are the results of arbitrary policies propounded by politicians and that other and better laws and policies are equally possible. At one level this is the story of a clash between two visions of what Orang Asli should become, their own vision and that of the Malaysian ruling class.

ORANG ASLI IN THE MALAYAN ETHNIC MOSAIC

Malaysia is a "plural society," meaning one made up of two or more culturally distinct and economically specialized ethnic groups. Malaysians are justifiably proud of the relative harmony between the different groups. Violent conflict between ethnic groups, common in the world today, is almost nonexistent in Malaysia. The only exception—a bloody clash between Chinese and Malays following Chinese election successes in May 1969—made such an imprint on the national psyche that the government reshaped its policies with the goal of preventing such an outbreak from ever recurring.

But the interethnic harmony in Malaysia is not due to ethnicity's having little importance in people's minds. In fact Malaysians think and act first and foremost as members of ethnic groups. Many scholars attribute the absence of class consciousness in Malaysia to the overriding strength of ethnic identity. Malaysians tend not to recognize either common economic interests with members of other ethnic groups or class differences within their own groups (Milne and Mauzy 1986:76-80; Rigg 1991:123).

Malaysian national life is dominated by competition between the major groups—Malays, Chinese, and Indians—in the political and economic arenas. While economic specialization by ethnic group is eroding, the major political parties are still ethnically-based. Malaysian harmony results from delicately balancing the interests of the major competing groups.

Orang Asli, who make up less than 1 percent of Peninsular Malaysia's 16 million people (in 1994), are profoundly affected by the larger groups and by the struggle between them. To understand what is happening to Orang Asli, then, it is necessary to know something about the dominant ethnic groups as well. In this section, therefore, we give a brief introduction to the Orang Asli followed by summary descriptions of the Malays, Chinese, and Indians. These dominant peoples form an important part of the Orang Asli's environment, and their cultures provide models, positive and negative, for Orang Asli.

Orang Asli

The Orang Asli, totaling about 90,000 people in 1995, are not a single ethnic group. They comprise at least nineteen distinct groups, varying in size from about 100 to 20,000 and differing in language, social organization, economy, religion, and physical characteristics. What these groups have in common is that they are non-Malay indigenous peoples, descendants of peoples who occupied the Malay Peninsula before the establishment of Malay kingdoms during the second millennium A.D. (The only exception are the Orang Kuala [also called Dossin Dolak or Duano], Muslim immigrants from Sumatra who specialize in sea fishing and strand foraging.) They live in scattered camps and villages in the high river valleys of the central mountain range, in the foothills and lowlands on both sides of the Peninsula, and in various locations along the coasts. Most groups speak Mon-Khmer languages—showing an ancient connection with mainland Southeast Asia to the north, where most Mon-Khmer languages are found—although a few of the more southerly groups have lost their aboriginal languages and now speak only Malay.

For the most part Orang Asli continue to follow indigenous religions, which are closely integrated with their environments and specific ways of life, but in recent years, according to government claims (*Berita Harian* 1993), about one in ten Orang Asli has converted to Islam, the religion of the politically dominant Malays.

Contemporary Orang Asli ways of life have roots deep in prehistory. Archaeological evidence strongly suggests that Orang Asli are direct descendants of the Hoabinhians, the earliest well-documented inhabitants of the Malay Peninsula (Rambo 1979:61; Solheim 1980; Bellwood 1985:159-75; Benjamin 1985; Adi 1985). Hoabinhinian sites, which can be identified by a characteristic set of pebble tools, have been found throughout mainland Southeast Asia and at a few places on the northeastern coast of the island of Sumatra. In the Malay Peninsula the dates of the sites range from 8000 B.C., the end of the last ice age, to about 1000 B.C. The Hoabinhians were probably nomadic foragers (hunter-gatherers), camping wherever they found food until the supplies were exhausted and then moving on. Judging by the teeth of Hoabinhian skeletons from Gua Cha in Kelantan, the people had "a well-balanced diet, with animal proteins, considerable fibrous starchy vegetables (especially wild yams), and a relatively large proportion of sweet foods, specifically fruits and honey" (Bulbeck 1985:97). The Hoabinhian sites near the west coast of the Peninsula show an economy adapted to coastal resources, especially shellfish.

In the second millennium B.C., a new culture replaced the Hoabinhian in the Peninsula (Bellwood 1985:258-70). This "neolithic" culture, a variant of the Ban Kao culture of western Thailand, is characterized by fine pottery and polished stone tools. The Malayan neolithic culture may have been introduced into the Peninsula by Mon-Khmer-speaking immigrants from modern-day Thailand who intermarried with the earlier Hoabinhians (Bellwood 1985:268-70). This would explain the sudden full-blown appearance of a Ban Kao-style culture in a Hoabinhian landscape and would provide the ultimate source of the Mon-Khmer languages still spoken by most Orang Asli. Probably the neolithic people grew some crops, though no remains of cultivated plants from before

A.D. 1100 have yet been found (Adi 1985:xi, 32, 35, 69). Many of the neolithic tools would have been suitable for use in farming. Crops probably included Southeast Asian cultigens like yams, rice, Job's tears, and foxtail millet (Tweedie 1953:61; Bellwood 1985:260, 268; Dentan 1968:47). Fruit trees were probably domesticated during this time.

The Hoabinhian foragers had little incentive to trade, for travel was difficult in the rainforest, and most groups had similar resources. But trade would have increased as economic systems in the Peninsula became more differentiated. Probably for some time after the introduction of the neolithic technology, crops, and farming techniques, many groups simply combined horticulture with their earlier foraging, but linguistic evidence suggests that by about 1000 B.C. groups had begun to specialize either in foraging or farming (Benjamin 1985:242-3, 261). This specialization probably generated the trade between foragers and farmers, found in historic times, of forest products, like resin for torches, in return for agricultural produce.

After about 1000 B.C. Austronesian-speaking seafarers, probably from Borneo and present-day Indonesia, began to settle in small numbers at the river mouths and along the southern coasts of the Peninsula (Bellwood 1985:258, 270). These people were traders as well as fishermen and farmers. During the first millennium A.D. traders from India, China, and the Mon civilizations of southern Thailand also reached the Peninsula. People in the interior became suppliers of forest products in demand in the outside world—resins, incense woods, rhinoceros horns, feathers, even gold (Dunn 1975; Benjamin 1985:261-2). Trade became important in the economies of many forest-dwelling groups, especially in the southern part of the Peninsula where the relatively flat terrain and slowly flowing rivers made travel between the coast and the interior easy. Apparently some southern Orang Asli adopted the Austronesian language (ancestral Malay?) of their trade partners and eventually assimilated into the Austronesian population, a process that has continued into this century (Benjamin 1985:244-7).

The basic economic activities in Malayan prehistory— hunting, fishing, gathering, strand foraging, farming, and trade—occur, with modifications, in the economies of contemporary Orang Asli. A few stable and coherent combinations of economic activities predominated before the recent incursions of development (Benjamin 1985). The inland Hoabinhian pattern of generalized foraging continued into this century among several small Orang Asli groups, including Kensiu, Kintaq, Jahai, Batek De', and Semaq Beri (see map and table). Unlike Hoabinhians, however, they collected forest products for trade as well as food. "Neolithic" swidden farming (but with metal tools), with minimal outside trade, was the basis of the economies of some more isolated Orang Asli, like east Semai, Temiar, Mendriq, Lanoh, Batek Nong, and Jah Hut. Some southerly and forest fringe groups—including the west Semai, Semelai, Orang Hulu (Jakun), and Temuan—practiced mixed horticulture (with an emphasis on tree crops) combined with trade. This pattern still characterizes the farming groups most in touch with the outside world and the market economy. Finally, like coastal Hoabinhians, a few groups (Orang Seletar, Orang Kuala, and Btsisi') specialized in harvesting the products of the sea, shore, and mangroves for their own consumption and for trade. These economic systems combined with appropriate social organizations and ideologies to form ideal-typical Orang Asli "ways of life." In the next chapter we describe four representative groups—Batek De', east Semai, west Semai, and Temuan—in some detail to show how these ways of life worked in practice.

The table inside the cover gives some basic facts about the various Orang Asli groups.

Malays

Numerically and politically Malays dominate Peninsular Malaysia. They were about 58 percent of the total population in 1989 (Rigg 1991:117). The Malaysian Federal Constitution, following colonial practice, defines a Malay as "one who speaks the Malay language, professes Islam and habitually follows Malay customs" (Andaya and Andaya 1982:302). These defining features have separate origins and histories, only coming together after the adoption of Sunni Islam by the ruler of the trading port of Malacca on the west coast of the Peninsula in the early fifteenth century. Malay was the language of the first rulers of Malacca, who, according to tradition, originated in southeastern Sumatra (perhaps at Melayu on the Jambi River). Malay spread as a trade language throughout the Indonesian archipelago and the Peninsula during the period in which Malacca ruled the seas. It gradually replaced the earlier Mon-Khmer languages of southerly Orang Asli groups.

The rulers of Malacca learned Islam from Arabs and Indian Muslims, who dominated Southeast Asian maritime trade from the thirteenth century onward. Rulers on both sides of the Peninsula adopted Islam, and it gradually spread to local people, displacing to some extent their earlier animistic and Hindu-Buddhist beliefs and practices. The resulting "Pasisir" culture of the ruling class was coastal, urban, mercantile, slavocratic, and oriented toward the sea and the Islamic West rather than toward the interior, where Orang Asli and Malay peasants lived.

Malay customs have been continually changing throughout recorded history. For example, in the last few decades ruling class Malays have condemned traditional Malay customs (like shadow-plays) and styles of dress (like women's *sarung kebaya*) as insufficiently Islamic. At the same time Western practices and habits have penetrated the ruling class Malay life-style. Still, a few distinctive features, such as elaborate politeness and deference to social superiors, remain vital.

Because official Malayness is defined by culture rather than descent, non-Malays can "become Malay" by adopting the identifying practices. Since today most Malaysians can speak Malay, and the truly distinctive Malay customs are few, religion has become the key criterion. Thus, adopting Islam is generally equated with "becoming a Malay" (*masuk Melayu*).

This flexibility of definition is ancient. Malays are of mixed ethnic origin (Nagata 1979), stemming ultimately from Austronesian-speaking traders, fishermen, and pirates who began settling the peninsular coasts after 1000 BC (Bellwood 1985:270). Muslim traders, mostly Indians and Arabs, married into the feudal ruling class, while their African, Indonesian, and Orang Asli slaves merged with their other subjects. Especially after British rule began, waves of immigrants from Indonesia descended upon local Malay peasants and Orang Asli: Javanese, Bugis from Sulawesi, and Sumatran peoples (Minangkabau, Rawas, Mandailing, Kerenci, Achenese), often overwhelming the indigenes, driving them into the hills or enslaving them (Andaya and Andaya 1982:180-181). As the struggle for independence from the British began, the Pasisir ruling class identified itself with these subject peoples of the interior as if they were all one ethnic group. In this effort, they took inspiration from their mentors, the British colonial regime, in whose official documents (e.g., the census) European racism conflated Orang Asli, local Malays, Indonesian immigrants, and the multi-ethnic ruling class into a spurious category called "Malay Population" (Anderson 1991:164-166). Although members of that "population" themselves continued, and continue, to distinguish between these ethnic groups, the restive feudal rulers and the rising Malay colonial bureaucracy claimed to represent this "Malay Population," creating popular support for "Malay" dominance in an independent state (Andaya and Andaya 1982:301-302; Dentan i.p.; Roff 1967). Thus, most Malays, like most Americans, can trace their origins to multiple sources.

Traditionally most ordinary Malays were coastal fishermen and traders or peasant farmers in the major river valleys and the broad coastal plains of the northern states of Kedah and Kelantan. Most still are. The peasants live in small villages (*kampung*), strung out along a riverbank or road, in small wooden houses with thatch or corrugated iron roofs, surrounded by coconut and fruit trees, ornamental plants, and kitchen gardens. Villagers grow a mixture of subsistence crops, like rice, and cash crops. They sell coffee beans and rubber to middlemen and sell surplus food in local farmers' markets. They raise chickens and goats to eat or sell. Some families keep water buffalo for ploughing. Land holdings are generally small, as the government encourages Malays to have large families, and all children inherit a share.

Nowadays many Malays work for the government, including the police and army. Special quotas favoring Malays in higher education and government hiring have led to Malays filling most jobs in the federal and state bureaucracies. Some educated Malays are in teaching and other professions. Some are in business, mostly in corporations and quasi-governmental enterprises. The government requires foreign corporations to hire Malay executives and managers.

Traditional Malay society included a hereditary ruling class, often of extrapeninsular origin, and a great mass of mostly local commoners (*orang biasa*). Now a still-small middle class is growing. The British colonial government retained the hereditary rulers as figureheads, and the Constitution confirms their positions and special privileges. Most Peninsular states still have sultans. The position of King rotates among these sultans for five-year terms. Malays still show respect and deference toward sultans. This deference has now expanded to include politicians and government officials. Those officials, in turn, often act in ways that strike Westerners as arrogant or condescending in their dealings with common people. The modern ruling class is no longer purely hereditary. People with educational or political qualifications may now enter it. But those in authority still hold the feudal attitude that it is their right to make decisions for those beneath them and subordinates' duty to obey and be grateful (Dentan i.p.).

Nowadays the dominant Malay political party, UMNO (United Malays National Organisation), argues that "Islamic" values should inform the laws and practices of the nation, but it does not support a theocratic state. The Constitution makes Islam the national religion, but guarantees freedom of religion (except to Malays). Many Malays say, however, that Malaysia should be an Islamic state, in which all laws and political and economic practices derive from the Quran and the Islamic law codes (*syaria*). The Islamic Party (PAS) propounds this view.

Orang Asli have far more contact with Malays than with the other major ethnic groups, the Chinese and Indians. Rural Orang Asli villages are often near Malay *kampung*s. Residents may meet at the farmers' markets and coffee shops in nearby towns, although Semai tend to cluster in particular shops where they can eat pork or drink beer in peace. Even deep forest-dwelling groups like the Batek have dealings with

Malay farmers and traders. Most government officials they meet are Malays, including JHEOA staff, police, game wardens, and forestry officers.

Orang Asli life exists in the shadow of Malay culture. Describing their own culture, Orang Asli persistently contrast how they do things with how Malays do them (e.g., Dentan 1976). Yet, despite and because of this pervasive opposing of the two ways of life, they tend to see the world through the filter of Malay culture (Hood Salleh 1984). For centuries Orang Asli have lived a fugitive existence, seduced or enslaved by an encroaching Malay civilization which they also resisted and fled.

Chinese

The largest ethnic minority in Peninsular Malaysia is Chinese, 31.8 percent in 1989 (Rigg 1991:117).[2] Although Malaysian Chinese descend from immigrants, like many Malays, most were born in Malaysia and are citizens by birth. There has been little recent migration either from or to China.

Most Chinese immigrants came during colonial rule between about 1830 and the great depression of the 1930s. The immigrants were peasants fleeing political turmoil and poverty in the southern maritime provinces of Kwantung and Fukien. They spoke several different languages. Some Chinese ventured into the interior, where they worked mostly in tin mining. By the early twentieth century some had moved into small-scale trade and shopkeeping and begun to put down roots. They married Chinese women and established families. The children of those families married each other, and by the 1930s the Malaysian Chinese community was largely self-perpetuating.

Most Chinese remain separate from the Malays socially and culturally. Intermarriage is rare, partly because many Malays will not accept Chinese spouses into their community even if they convert to Islam.

---

2. The classic source on the Malayan Chinese is Purcell (1948). Other useful sources include Heider (1974) and Mabbett and Mabbett (1972). Most works on Malaysian history, politics, and economics provide information on the Chinese.

Most Chinese live in cities and towns. A few are commercial farmers in rural areas, like the Cameron Highlands in west Semai country. Even in heavily Malay states like Kedah and Kelantan, towns and cities have a strong Chinese flavor. The older streets are lined with continuous rows of Chinese shophouses, usually two-story wood and masonry structures with tile roofs, sometimes with ornately carved shutters and trim on the upper story, which extends out over the sidewalk creating a covered walkway below. The ground floor shops open directly onto the sidewalk. Traditionally the upper floor was the living quarters for the extended family that owned the shop. Wealthier businessmen and professionals usually live in the suburbs.

Chinese dominate commerce. Small businessmen tend to be opportunistic, often pursuing several ventures—retailing, wholesaling, trading, manufacturing, etc.—at once. Most Chinese farmers are cash-croppers rather than subsistence growers. Chinese who do not own their own businesses or participate in a family business usually work for wages. Recently some Chinese have moved into teaching, journalism, and other professions that require extensive education. Hiring preferences for Malays keep most Chinese out of government service.

In preparing for independence, the leaders of the Malay, Chinese, and Indian communities made an agreement, known as the "Bargain."

> The essence of the Bargain was the acceptance by the non-Malay leaders that the Malays, as the indigenous race, were entitled to political dominance, while in return the Malay leaders recognized that the socioeconomic pursuits of the non-Malays should not be infringed upon. (Milne and Mauzy 1986:28)

By the late 1960s the economic gap between Chinese and Malays had widened, creating resentment which was partly responsible for the violent clashes between Chinese and Malays in May 1969. After these clashes the government established the New Economic Policy (NEP) to reduce poverty and to distribute income and wealth more equitably between the two groups. Under the NEP, which is still in force, the government instituted numerous measures and agencies aimed at improving the economic position of Malays (Rigg 1991:116-127). While the NEP has had some success in alleviating poverty and has created a group of wealthy Malays, it has handicapped Chinese businessmen and Chinese citizens in general. But the overall growth of the Malaysian economy since 1970 has allowed most Chinese to prosper, though not necessarily at levels they would like.

Despite the "Bargain" of 1957, Malaysian Chinese remain active in local and national politics. Leaders of "clans" (groups with common surnames) are influential in Chinese areas. Three predominantly Chinese parties—the Malaysian Chinese Association (MCA), the People's Progressive Party (PPP), and Gerakan—belong to the ruling coalition, the National Front (*Barisan Nasional*), dominated by the United Malays National Organization (UMNO). A major opposition party, the Democratic Action Party (DAP), is also mainly Chinese and represents a Chinese point of view.

Orang Asli contact with Chinese is largely economic. They sometimes sell products to Chinese middlemen, work in Chinese enterprises like tea estates, and buy things from Chinese shops. The only credit available to most Orang Asli is that which Chinese extend to people who work for or trade with them. Despite some exploitation, there is enough mutual benefit that business relationships between Chinese and Orang Asli are common throughout the Peninsula. Most Orang Asli have a rather positive attitude toward Chinese. Chinese do not openly ridicule them or pressure them to change their ways of living, as many Malays do. Like Orang Asli, Chinese eat pork and have no fasting month. There is even some intermarriage between Chinese and Orang Asli; usually a Chinese man—a logger or farmer—marries an Orang Asli woman and settles down with her group. Some of these "marriages" end, however, when the man moves on.

Indians

The third major ethnic group is the Indians, 8 percent of the Peninsular Malaysian population in 1989 (Rigg 1991:117).

Most Malaysian Indians are Hindu Tamils from southern India, who were brought by the British after the mid-nineteenth century to serve as cheap plantation workers (Arasaratnam 1979). They live predominantly on the west coast, a quarter in Selangor state alone. Even today almost half of all Indians are impoverished tappers and laborers living on rubber and oil palm plantations. Some Indians work as laborers for government agencies, a few are businessmen, and some are professionals, especially lawyers and doctors. Many Indians support the Malaysian Indian Congress (MIC), a minor party in the ruling coalition, and others are active in Chinese-dominated parties, like Gerakan and the opposition DAP.

Except for Btsisi' who are being squeezed out by oil palm plantations manned by Tamils, Orang Asli today have little contact with Indians. However, elements of Hindu and Buddhist cosmology and mythology, such as the belief in an enormous snake (*naga*) under the earth, persist in some Orang Asli religions and show at least indirect Indian influence in earlier days.

CLAIMS TO INDIGENOUS STATUS

> "When *I* use a word," Humpty Dumpty said, in rather a scornful tone, "it means just what I choose it to mean—neither more nor less."
>
> "The question is," said Alice, "whether you *can* make words mean so many different things."
>
> "The question is," said Humpty Dumpty, "which is to be master—that's all."
>
> Lewis Carroll, *Through the Looking-Glass*

Under the Federal Constitution (Article 153) the King is responsible for safeguarding the "special position" of the Malays and the natives of Malaysian Borneo. He is to reserve for them a "reasonable" proportion of scholarships, positions in the federal public service, places in educational institutions, and licenses for trade or business. The government uses this provision to try to increase the number of Malays and natives in business and the professions and thereby to improve their economic position relative to the Chinese. In practice this allocation benefits mostly Malays. For instance, they receive four out of every five positions in the public service (Mahathir 1970:76).

The rationale for these special rights is that the Malays and Bornean natives are "indigenous peoples," in contrast to Chinese and Indian descendants of immigrants. Malays and Bornean natives are termed *bumiputera*, a Sanskrit-derived term meaning "princes of the soil." According to the current Prime Minister, Mahathir Mohamad, "the Malays are the original or indigenous people of Malaya and the only people who can claim Malaya as their one and only country" (1970:133). Yet the United Nations defines indigenous peoples as follows:

> Indigenous populations are composed of the existing descendants of the peoples who inhabited the present territory of a country wholly or partially at the time when persons of a different culture or ethnic origin arrived there from other parts of the world, overcame them and, by conquest, settlement or other means, reduced them to a non-dominant or colonial situation; who today live more in conformity with their particular social, economic and cultural customs and traditions than with the institutions of the country of which they now form a part, under a State structure which incorporates mainly the national, social and cultural characteristics of other segments of the population which are predominant. (Burger 1987:6-7)

According to this widely accepted definition, the Malay claim to being indigenous is shaky. Certainly *some* ancestors of the Malays arrived before the British, Chinese, and Indians. Probably Austronesian-speakers have lived in the Peninsula for 3000 years, longer than the Anglo-Saxons have been in Britain. But considering the massive influx of ancestral Malays into the Peninsula in the second millennium A.D., they can equally well be seen as conquerors or colonizers who gained political control over the indigenous Orang Asli. The

Malaysian government claims that only it has the right to define who the indigenous peoples of Malaysia are,[3] an assertion which tells more about the hegemonic power of the government than about the facts of the case. The government has made it illegal to question the claim that Malays are indigenous, on the grounds that to do so would cause friction between ethnic communities.

The Orang Asli, while generally acknowledged as the earliest inhabitants of the Malay Peninsula, are not included in the category of peoples having special rights, the *bumiputera* [4]. The government has not explained the reasons for their exclusion, but a discussion by Prime Minister Mahathir (1970:126-127) sheds some light on the matter.

> The first conclusion from the study of other countries is that the presence of aborigines prior to settlement by other races does not mean that the country is internationally recognized as belonging to the aborigines. Aborigines are found in Australia, Taiwan and Japan, to name a few, but nowhere are they regarded as the definitive people of the country concerned. The definitive people are those who set up the first governments and these governments were the ones with which other countries did official business and had diplomatic relations.
>
> There is another condition. The people who form the first effective Government and their legal successors must at all times outnumber the original tribes found in a given country. . . .
>
> In Malaya, the Malays without doubt formed the first effective governments. . . . The *Orang Melayu* or

---

3. Statement by the current Deputy Prime Minister, Anwar bin Ibrahim to the "International Seminar on Indigenous People," sponsored by the Malaysian Ministry of Culture, Arts, and Tourism (Kuala Lumpur, November 29-December 1, 1993).
4. As we discuss in Chapter 3, the government treats Orang Asli as *bumiputera* for some purposes, but does not give them the special privileges granted Malays and natives of Sabah and Sarawak by the Federal Constitution.

Malays have always been the definitive people of the Malay Peninsula. The aborigines were never accorded any such recognition nor did they claim such recognition. There was no known aborigine government or aborigine state. Above all, at no time did they outnumber the Malays.[5]

This passage rationalizes the Malaysian government's rejection of Orang Asli as the owners and rightful rulers of Malaysia, but it does not justify their being denied the special rights intended to advance indigenous peoples. We return to this question in Chapter 3.

---

5. For a similar view by Malaysia's first Prime Minister, Tunku Abdul Rahman, see *New Straits Times*, November 6, 1986 .

2

Orang Asli Before Development

Before the mid 1950s most Orang Asli lived in relative isolation from the three main forces of "modernization": government-sponsored development projects,
government political control, and the market economy.
They were economically self-sufficient and politically
independent. They engaged the outside world when
and how they wished. This isolation began to break
down in colonial times, as plantations and tin mines
sprang up in Orang Asli areas. It crumbled entirely
after Malaysia's independence. But some groups were
relatively independent recently enough that the
present authors could study them in that condition,
although the market economy already affected these
groups to varying degrees. To provide a baseline for
measuring the benefits and costs of modernization for
Orang Asli, we briefly describe in this chapter the ways
of life of four representative groups before the full
impact of government-sponsored development and
control.

BATEK: FORAGER-TRADERS OF THE LOWLAND RAINFOREST (1975-1976)[1]

The Batek De' are a Semang or "Malayan Negrito" group, characterized by small stature, dark skin, and curly hair. Their language is in the Northern Aslian division of the Aslian family of Mon-Khmer languages. They live in the watershed of the Lebir River in Kelantan state and along the northern tributaries of the Tembeling River in adjacent parts of Pahang state. Their total population is about 700.

Before the massive logging and development of oil palm plantations of the 1970s and 1980s, Kelantan Batek lived in the rainforest in small groups. They made their living by hunting, gathering, and trading rattan and *gaharu* (a resinous wood used in perfume and incense) for such things as rice, tobacco, cloth, and iron tools. They lived in temporary camps, typically of twenty to forty people. Each nuclear family had its own lean-to, about five by seven feet, made of poles and palm-leaf thatch. Inside a slightly raised platform, made of split bamboo on a log base, formed the family's bed and sitting place. Usually adolescents, too big to fit into the family shelter, shared one or more shelters of their own. Under the low side of the lean-to roof people stored rolled-up pandanus leaf sleeping mats, blankets, clothes, cooking pots, blowpipes, darts, and other possessions. The family cooking fire was kept smoldering just under the front edge of the thatch. Shelters often were clustered together, forming a communal workspace between them, but the form of the camps varied according to local terrain. Camps were always near a river or stream—which served as water source, laundry, bathing place, and, downstream, toilet—and convenient to sources of food and trade goods.

Camps were the centers of communal life. In the mornings work parties formed and set out on their tasks. Some adults stayed in camp all day, making blowpipe darts, weaving pandanus mats or baskets, cooking, and minding small

---

1. Kirk Endicott did research with Batek in 1971-1973, 1975-1976, 1981, and 1990. For further information on Batek, see Endicott 1979a, 1984; Karen Endicott 1979.

children who played noisily in the shelters, stream, and nearby trees. In the evenings work parties returned with food or forest produce, parents prepared food for their families, and people gradually settled down for the night. Conversations and singing might continue well after dark. Sometimes singing and trancing ceremonies were carried out in the coolness of the night, when, people said, superhuman beings felt comfortable descending to earth.

During the mid 1970s Batek got about half their food from hunting and gathering and half from trading forest produce (Endicott 1984). Typically a man—but sometimes a woman without small children—would make an agreement with one of the Malay traders who periodically came into the forest by boat. The Batek would agree to supply a certain quantity of rattan by a certain date in return for an agreed amount of goods or cash. The trader usually gave an advance in the form of food and tobacco and then paid off the remainder upon delivery of the rattan. Sometimes different members of a camp made agreements with different traders. Then the group would move to an area where the rattan had not been recently harvested and would begin collecting.

All Batek had the right to live and work anywhere within their traditional territory, usually the drainage basin of a particular river or stream. People knew the resources of their territories well and moved to favored areas as different foods came into season.

Food and other resources were free to all Batek and only became personal property after being collected. During the first few weeks of a contract, which might last a month or six weeks, people ate rice and flour (usually as fried dough) together with fish, game, honey, and wild fruits and vegetables. When trade foods ran out, they switched to eating wild yams as their staple carbohydrate. They shared both traded and foraged foods throughout the camp, so no one went hungry unless everyone did. People normally varied their activities from day to day, depending on opportunities and individual interests. Thus, on any given day a few people, usually mature men, would go out blowpipe hunting, a group of men and women might collect rattan, and a group composed mostly of women and children might go out looking for wild yams. Others might stay in camp doing chores or perhaps do a little fishing with hook and line in the nearby stream. During fruit season, work parties would go to the trees, cut down the fruit, and bring it back. Similarly, honey season would see parties, mostly of men and adolescents of both sexes, set out at dusk for a bee tree. There they would smoke the bees out of their nests, which hang from the upper limbs of tall trees, and bring back the honey, wax, and larvae.

By being flexible enough to change activities and locations to take advantage of constantly changing opportunities, Batek obtained a healthy diet as well as most trade goods they wanted without working more than about thirty hours per person per week. They kept material possessions down to what they could comfortably carry.

Batek camps were collections of autonomous nuclear families (a husband, wife, and their children). Camp composition changed almost daily as some families left to join other camps and other families moved in. When an entire camp moved, component families might split up and form more than one new camp, or some families might join other camps. Within families, husbands and wives together decided where to live and what to do. Neither sex had greater authority or prestige than the other (Karen Endicott 1979). Marriages were not arranged; they rested on personal attraction, and, if that faltered, either spouse could initiate a divorce simply by leaving. Although all camp members were usually related to each other by kinship, through one or both parents, or through marriage ties, families had no obligation to camp with particular relatives. An exception was the obligation adult children felt to camp with and help their aged parents. This duty might informally rotate among siblings.

Camp leadership beyond the nuclear family was weak or nonexistent. Sometimes a camp contained a recognizable natural leader, even one appointed "headman" (*penghulu*) by the JHEOA, but their power was limited to persuasion. Personality, not gender or hereditary ties, determined who the leaders were. A woman, Tanyogn, headed the group the Endicotts stayed with in 1975-1976. She was remarkably capable and persuasive—an expert in herbal medicine and most traditional crafts and a formidable debater—but, like male leaders, she lacked formal authority, even over her own adult children. Few camp-wide activities required coordination by a leader. Most activities were so familiar that everyone just pitched in, as in poisoning fish in a side-stream. In others people simply followed the lead of whoever was most expert at that activity, as in singing ceremonies.

Batek values supported their flexible social organization and economy. Everyone, even children, had a right to personal autonomy. Using threats and especially physical coercion on someone was regarded as intolerable. People said that the group would abandon anyone who acted aggressively or violently toward others. Violent acts were rare, and no one could remember anyone being abandoned. Children were expected to respect their elders, but not necessarily to obey them. Coupled with the value on personal autonomy was an equally strong obligation to help others whenever help was needed. This was expressed most vividly in the obligation to share all food throughout the camp, an obligation acted out daily. Similarly, people spontaneously helped orphans, older people, blind, sick, or otherwise handicapped people. Batek knew they had to cooperate to survive. Selfish or thoughtless behavior threatened the group. People who had been offended or neglected might suffer from a psychosomatic disease, called ke'oy, characterized by fits of uncontrolled sobbing. In a case of ke'oy, the group would bring moral pressure to bear on the offender to make amends, an essential component of the cure, thus re-asserting the need for mutual consideration among members of the camp.

Batek religion was a complex set of beliefs and rituals that gave meaning to their existence and provided means for dealing with the forces of nature that impinged on their lives (Endicott 1979a). Batek believed that there were worlds above the firmament and below the earth, populated by immortal superhuman beings (hala'), some of whom existed from the beginning of time and others who derived from the shadow-souls of deceased Batek. The primordial superhumans were creator beings with a continuing responsibility to maintain cosmic order and natural processes, like the annual cycle of fruit and honey seasons. Human responsibility was to observe an elaborate set of prohibitions on such acts as having sex with close relatives, mixing certain categories of foods, and mocking various species of animals, acts which would undermine the cosmic order. Batek said that if they respected the superhumans and followed the prohibitions, the superhumans would reward them with abundant fruit harvests, good health, and general well-being. If anyone broke a prohibition, the thunder-god, Gobar, who lives on a giant stone pillar reaching from the earth to the sky world, would send a violent storm which would topple huge trees over the offender's camp. The thunder-god might also enlist an underground deity, pictured variously as an old woman or huge snake, to cause an eruption of the underground sea that would dissolve the earth beneath the offender's camp. To ward off storm and flood, offenders should make a blood sacrifice by lightly cutting the skin on one shin, mixing the blood with some water, and throwing the mixture to the sky and the earth to assuage the angry deities.

To maintain good relations with the superhumans, Batek communicated with them regularly through singing sessions in which shamans might go into trance and send their shadow-souls to visit the superhumans. At the beginning and end of fruit seasons, people built low platforms of tree bark on logs, covered by a huge lean-to roof of thatch. There they sang to the superhumans, first, to ask for abundant fruit and, later, to thank them for sending it. After a death, to ensure that the deceased's shadow-soul could join the superhumans atop the firmament, Batek placed the corpse on a platform in a tree and burned incense beside it, so the shadow-soul could follow the smoke to the sky.

During the 1980s and early 1990s the entire Lebir River valley outside the National Park (Taman Negara) was logged off and turned into oil palm and rubber plantations. Some Batek settled at Post Lebir, a government settlement, but most retreated into Taman Negara, where they have tried to continue their former life (see Chapter 5).

EAST SEMAI: UPLAND SWIDDEN FARMERS (1962)[2]

Semai are the largest single group of Orang Asli, numbering over 19,000 in 1986. They live in a large area on both sides of the Perak-Pahang border (see Map), from isolated valleys in the central mountain range to the western foothills in Perak. Semai resemble other Southeast Asian hill peoples, being less than five and a half feet tall with golden brown skin and black wavy hair. Their language, which is in the Central Aslian division of Mon-Khmer, contains forty-odd dialects, because their settlements are scattered and the rugged terrain makes communication between them difficult. Although Semai share many fundamental beliefs and attitudes, there are also major cultural variations among different groups. Until recently they did not think of themselves as an "ethnic group," only as "not-Malays," people whom Malays treated with contempt, a sort of negative ethnicity. Like most peoples of the world, Semai called themselves simply "people," *sn'ooy* or *sng'ooy*, terms which Europeans wrote as Senoi or Sengoi. They also called themselves "hill people," "forest people," "poor people," people of a particular river basin, and so on. In the 1960s Semai in the Perak foothills called Semai in the Pahang mountains "those Temiar" (another Orang Asli people); Pahang Semai called those in Perak "those Malays." These perceptions reflect the differences between "east Semai" ways of life, based on swidden ("slash-and-burn") farming, and "west Semai" ways, dependent on a mixture of subsistence farming and production of commodities (Dentan 1968; Gomes 1986). These two economic systems, which we call "swiddening" and "mixed horticulture" for short, involve distinct social arrangements, political systems, and outlooks on life.

In 1962 east Semai exemplified the swiddening way of life. They were just recovering from the disruption of a Communist insurgency (the "Emergency"). Anti-government

---

2. Robert K. Dentan lived with and studied east Semai for seven months in 1961-1962. For further information on east Semai, see Dentan 1968, Fix 1977, and Nicholas 1994.

guerrillas had roamed through their homelands. The colonial government had tried to remove Semai from Communist influence by resettling them in concentration camps outside the forest, causing many deaths and enormous anxiety. When the folly of resettlement became obvious, east Semai were allowed to return to their homes along the upper reaches of the rivers that drained the main mountain range. As the guerrilla threat receded, they regained some autonomy. They became self-sufficient in food production again, although they carried on limited trade with the outside world—as they had for centuries. "Without iron and salt, we would weep," said an elder. "But we don't need the other stuff."

Settlements typically consisted of six or eight houses, some clustered together on riverside hilltops or ridges which had been cleared of vegetation and others scattered near the fields. Most houses were flimsy affairs with pole frames, split bamboo floors and walls, and thatched roofs, raised a few feet above the ground on posts to keep them cool, dry, and relatively vermin-free. Such structures usually housed one or two nuclear families. But most villages had at least one larger and sturdier house holding several nuclear families, as many as fifty-four persons in a house. About a quarter of the east Semai settlements consisted of a single longhouse with family compartments along the sides and a central, rectangular common area for cooking and dancing. The larger houses formed refuges for the entire community in case of violent thunderstorms or invasions by tigers, elephants, or human attackers.

Every few years, when all the nearby arable land had been used, the people would abandon the settlement. Some families split off to join other groups, but most moved a few miles up- or down-river and built new houses near their new fields. Misunderstanding this patterned movement causes people sometimes to call Semai and other Orang Asli swiddeners "nomads."

The east Semai settlement pattern, like other features of Semai culture, may be an adaptation to pressure from Malays moving inland from the west coast. As their population increased, Malay swidden farmers gradually spread up the rivers, displacing the Semai already living there. This encroachment was facilitated by settlers or immigrant Malays who raided Semai settlements, slaughtering the men and taking the younger women and children back to sell or to use as domestic servants (see Chapter 3). Although slave raids ended by 1920, even in the 1960s many Semai still remembered them. The Semai response to raids was to flee ever further into the sparsely inhabited interior, scattering themselves in small groups in inaccessible places. Whenever groups of Semai came down from the hills to trade, they were careful to conceal the way back to their settlements, walking in streams to erase their tracks, lest slave raiders follow them back.

The core of the east Semai economy until recently was swiddening. People would cut down the trees and brush in a patch of forest, burn the dried vegetation to clear the ground and provide ash for fertilizer, and plant their crops in the cleared area (the "swidden"). After a year or two, when weeds and fast-growing second-growth shrubs and seedlings had invaded the clearing and overwhelmed the remaining crops, they abandoned the field and let it regenerate forest. The people then cleared another patch of forest and started the cycle again.

In the 1960s, east Semai cleared new plots every year, even though the previous year's clearing would still be producing some food in the form of longer-lasting vegetables, such as tapioca. In the relatively dry period between April and June, each family or group of related families chose a new plot for clearing. Advanced second growth forest was preferred, because the trees were big enough to provide substantial amounts of ash, but not so big that they were hard to cut down. Before starting to clear the chosen plot, a group member would perform a ritual in which he cleared a small patch of earth, cleansed it with magical water, and planted a small stick. If he had an auspicious dream that night or if the stick appeared to have grown by the next day, Semai thought the land was fertile. Usually groups of women and children began the clearing by slashing down the undergrowth with machetes. That took about a month. Then teams of men felled the trees with small steel-bladed axes. Whenever possible they would partially cut a group of trees and then fell a larger tree on top of them, knocking them all down like dominoes. This was great fun as well as labor-saving. Cleared trees and brush were left to dry for four to six weeks. Then, preferably after several days without rain, a few men would make torches and set the debris alight. If conditions were ripe, the fire would sweep up the slope and consume all the dead vegetation; if not, the men might have to pile up the unburned branches and logs and repeat the process. After burning, the soil cooled several days before planting. Fields prepared this way would look distinctly unpromising to an Iowa farmer—usually being situated on steep slopes and crisscrossed with charred tree-trunks—but the process served its intended purpose of baring and fertilizing the earth and exposing it to the sun and rain.

Before planting, "field heads" performed a ritual, which included planting fragrant magical plants to encourage the crops to grow. Planting was done by sizable groups of people of both sexes and all ages. Usually a group of men and boys, armed with long pointed poles, would walk ahead, punching shallow holes in the ground as they walked. A group of women and girls followed, dropping seeds, cuttings, or seedlings into the holes. Rice, the most favored staple crop, was planted first, often in the center of the clearing. Some days later, a patch of maize might be planted beside the rice and a wide border of tapioca around the edge of the clearing. Various minor crops—such as peppers, squash, chives, lemongrass, and tobacco—would be planted wherever the soil and other conditions suited them. The resulting disorderly jumble of crops contrasts sharply with the neat rows of a Western garden, but it has the advantage of inhibiting pests by breaking up the patches of each crop. A few diligent farmers weeded their fields as the crops grew, but most depended on the crops' head start to keep them above the weeds. East Semai occasionally planted perennial fruit trees, but they more often encouraged wild ones by clearing away competing vegetation, and they harvested the fruits when they came in season. By planting a great variety of crops and promoting wild fruit trees, Semai insured themselves against famine in case any one crop failed.

Crops ripened in sequence: first amaranth, then maize, squash, and finally rice. The most important root crop, tapioca, could be left in the ground until needed, but other crops had to be harvested when ripe and then eaten or stored. The rice harvest was a festive occasion. After a brief ceremony, groups of women would move through the field cutting off the rice ears with machetes or special small "rice knives," which could be concealed in the hand so they would not frighten the "soul" of the rice. They then spread the ears of rice on pandanus mats to dry, after which young men or women trod on them to separate the grains from the stalks. They would then store the rice in baskets in the houses. Before cooking the rice, women would pound it, using a wooden pestle and a mortar carved out of a log, and then winnow it with woven bamboo winnowing trays, allowing the breeze to blow the chaff away. Rice was boiled in metal pots or bamboo tubes and served with a side dish of fish, meat, or vegetables. The other staple, tapioca root, was boiled, roasted over the fire, or grated and baked as "bread."

Most protein in the east Semai diet came from fish and game. Their crops attracted pests like birds, deer, wild pigs, and elephants. Semai set many kinds of traps near the crops, which both protected the crops and supplied welcome meat to the diet. They hunted small game with blowpipes and poisoned darts and fished with baskets, nets, and hook and line. Some families raised a few chickens to be eaten on special occasions. Their highly varied diet, though low in protein, was generally adequate. Among essential nutrients, it lacked only iodine, as evidenced by the common occurrence of goiters.

There were no taboos against a man's doing woman's work or vice versa. Men did things that took upper body strength or involved leaving the settlement for long periods. Women said they were afraid to leave the settlement except in large groups, for fear of being kidnapped or raped "by Malays." There were far fewer women shamans than men, because, people said, being a shaman takes a lot out of you physically; far more midwives were women than men, because "women are used to giving birth." Midwives and shamans often married and worked together, or substituted for each other. Which one was called to treat a particular disease depended on the diagnosis of the disease.

The traditional rights of east Semai over land were not exclusive or permanent, a fact that made it hard for them to resist the incursions of outsiders armed with legal deeds, logging permits, or other government documents. Every Semai belonged to a band, a group of people who saw each other often and usually lived in a single settlement. Each band had a definable territory, usually both sides of a stretch of river, the band's "land" (*tei'*). People had strong sentimental ties to these lands, ties derived from having been born there, living there, and having buried kinsmen there. However, anyone, band member or not, could clear a field in a band's land. Whoever cleared the land had special rights over it until it lay fallow again. Usually several families cleared a field cooperatively and then marked off the individual family plots within it. Those plots belonged to the families who farmed them, but only as long as they were producing food. After that they became available for others.

Although food belonged to the families who produced it, east Semai, like the Batek, had to share it. Couples fed their own families first, but were expected to share any surplus with the rest of the household and then with the inhabitants of other houses, depending on the amount available. A hunter who killed a large animal—a pig or a python, say—shared it with every family in his settlement. Calculating gains and losses in this food sharing was against the rules. It was also tabu to refuse to share or, conversely, to ask someone for more than that person could spare. Semai said that frustrating people's needs, like hunger, could make them sick or accident prone. Sharing was an obligation, not a discretionary act, to be done in a matter-of-fact manner. Thanking an acquaintance was insulting, for it suggested that you were calculating the amount of the gift and that you did not expect the donor to be so generous. Distributing food by sharing kept food from spoiling and also cemented the entire settlement into a mutually supportive community. "Feeding" (*-prca'*) people, to the Semai way of thinking, stood for nurturance and love. Refusing to feed people stood for enmity, which people as vulnerable as Semai could not afford.

East Semai, again like Batek, respected the autonomy of the individual and the nuclear family, but they also tried to establish enduring cooperative ties with consanguines ("blood" relatives) and affines (marriage relatives) outside the family. They tended to see the world as hostile and their circle of consanguines as an oasis in a desert of dangerous strangers (*maay*). Households often consisted of extended families: either an older couple and one or more of their married children with their families, or two or more married siblings and their families. In longhouses, closely related families typically had side-by-side compartments and shared a common hearth. House groups formed the basis of the work groups that carried out farming activities and other economic tasks. House groups also cooperated in caring for children.

Forbidden to marry consanguines, east Semai usually had to seek partners outside their band, among the dreaded *maay*. After "marriage," which was marked simply by the couple moving in together and accepting the responsibilities of their married roles, the couple would live for a short time with the wife's relatives, then for a while with his, and then back with hers, gradually increasing the interval until they finally settled down at whichever location they liked best. In this way the partners slowly lost their fear and suspicion of their spouse's relatives, and their children grew up feeling at home with both parents' groups and territories. Extended sexual rights between in-laws further cemented ties. Although people had to show great respect and deference (what anthropologists call an "avoidance relationship") to all in-laws older than their spouses, especially opposite sex parents-in-law, relations between a spouse's younger siblings and the elder sibling's spouse were free and easy (a "joking relationship"). Husbands had the right to sleep with their wife's younger sisters, and wives could sleep with their husband's younger brothers, relationships that could develop into marriage if one spouse died. This practice not only tied the in-law groups together, but provided a sexual outlet for men while their wives were observing the two-year prohibition on sex after giving birth and for women when their husbands were away for extended periods.

Traditionally, Semai decided on issues of common concern by holding long meetings at which everyone got to voice his or her opinion until a consensus did or did not emerge. In some ways, inconclusive meetings which exhausted the participants were as good a way to reduce tensions as those at which one or the other party confessed to being in the wrong. East Semai women spoke up as freely at these meetings as the men did. The most influential voices were usually those of a few older men, for it was a fundamental principle of Semai social relations that one must respect those older than oneself. But even the revered elders had no coercive power. Individuals decided for themselves whether to follow the advice of the elders or abide by the group consensus.

The only person with a modicum of authority was the headman, a position that Malay traders and British colonial officials created for their own convenience. From the outsiders' viewpoint Semai participatory democracy took too long to arrive at decisions, which were not binding on anyone anyway. They "knew" that "savages" were ruled by "headmen," and that "headmen" must be men. Finding no such position, they invented one. By the 1960s, each band had an official headman with an official "letter of authority" (surat kuasa). This tie to powerful outsiders gave the man selected more clout than the other elders with whom he had previously been more or less equal. Perhaps he could protect the people, they thought, from outsider violence.

One of the most striking facets of Semai society was and is its nonviolence. Ethnographers from a wide variety of backgrounds and with a wide variety of interests have worked with Semai and related peoples. All, in one way or another, have had to deal with this nonviolence, however irrelevant it seemed to their original research topic. Many Semai find this fascination puzzling and a bit tiresome: puzzling, because it is not something that Semai think much about; and tiresome, because their neighbors take peaceability as a sign of timidity and weakness, a green light for expropriating Semai orchards and land. Semai are not incapable of violence. They just think that most violence is dangerous and stupid, and they act accordingly.

Semai peaceability was embedded in a pervasive egalitarianism. Forcing people to do something they did not want to, Semai said, ran the risk of making them sick or accident-prone. "Fetch some water," you say to your little girl. "I don't feel like it," she says. And there the discussion stops. To nag or bully the child would risk making her sick, maybe killing her. Of course you would not consider hitting her except under extreme circumstances.

As befitted a beleaguered people, east Semai notions of cosmology were full of dread. The cosmic order was fragile. Horrors always threatened to break through from the dark dimensions they inhabited and devour the people. Always Semai had to be careful what they said and did. "It's walking a narrow path," says Bah Tony, a Semai political leader. Normality could easily slip into perversion. Failure to observe proper behavior between people, or between people and animals, could unleash unspeakable supernatural retribution. A minor loss of self-restraint could make a whole settlement sink into the muddy waters beneath the earth; people could point out the sinkholes. "Thunder"—a sexually depraved, stupid, vicious destroyer who had to be shamed into leaving people alone—attacked settlements where people were careless about mixing categories of food. Bird demons, sometimes in the form of incubi or succubi, haunted people, especially pregnant and menstruating women. Tree spirits lay in wait for hunters. Appearances deceived.

Still, some people could establish a sort of parent-child/husband-wife relationship with some of these demons. Shamans and some midwives had familiars, who loved them and would help them. Hunters needed spirit "hunting wives" in the forest if they were to be successful. These familiars appeared in special dreams and gave the dreamer a melody which would later summon them to seances held in the dark.

H. D. Noone and Kilton Stewart, the first English-speakers to spend significant amounts of time with Semai and Temiar, found the transformation of demon into lover or child beguiling. They developed the idea, which Stewart subsequently popularized in the United States, that "Senoi" (the word for "person" in both languages) were able to achieve nonviolence, socioeconomic equality, perfect mental health, and so on simply by learning to control their dreams, turning a dream-threat into the donor of a spiritual gift.[3] Under the name "Senoi dream therapy," Stewart's notions of psychotherapy gained a modest following in the 1970s in the United States. Although most proponents understand that Stewart's description of "Senoi" dream practice is idealized and garbled, they note, correctly, that it has provided solace for troubled people.

Outsiders have now logged off and taken the land of the east Semai. The government has resettled most east Semai in "regroupment" villages (see Chapter 5).

WEST SEMAI: TRADER-HORTICULTURISTS OF THE FOOTHILLS (1963-1993)[4]

About 40 percent of Orang Asli today are rural peasants, not deep forest dwellers. That percentage will increase as logging, "development," and forced "regroupment" advance into the interior. These people have economies partially devoted to subsistence and partially to supplying commodities and labor to the market economy. This pattern grew out of the ancient combination of horticultural subsistence and trade in forest produce, a pattern which probably began in the first millennium B.C. In the case of the west Semai, who adopted this pattern only in this century, it seems to result from two conditions: increased contact with outsiders and loss of land. Contact with outsiders has exposed them to attractive goods obtainable only by purchase or trade. Loss of land has made it impossible to survive on their crops alone, thus necessitating trade for food.

3. Stewart's most accurate account is his Ph.D. thesis, "Magico-Religious Beliefs and Practises in Primitive Society—A Sociological Interpretation of Their Therapeutic Aspects" (1948). His most influential popular account is the article "Dream Theory in Malaya" (1972).
4. Robert K. Dentan did research with west Semai in 1962-1963, 1974, and 1991-1992. Alberto Gomes studied west Semai in 1982-1984 and 1986-1988. For further information on west Semai, see Dentan 1968; Khor 1985; Gomes 1986, 1989.

The west Semai settlement pattern reflects their orientation toward outside trade. Compact, semi-permanent villages, which contain 30-250 persons and average about 90, are located at intervals along the roads that climb into the mountains, interspersed with Malay villages. Groves of rubber and fruit trees surround each village. Sometimes the hillsides are dotted with swiddens at various stages of regeneration. Some villages also have a few rice paddies in low lying areas. Nuclear families generally live in separate, single-family houses, modeled on those of rural Malays (Hooker 1967). Some houses have plank floors and walls and corrugated iron roofs instead of thatch. A few rich families even have concrete-walled houses with tiled roofs and glass windows. The houses of closely related families may cluster together, forming homestead groups similar to the house groups that live together in the larger east Semai houses.

Villagers comprise two categories of people: descendants (through one or both parents) of the village founders and outsiders who have married into that group. All village residents have rights in the village territory (*lngrii'*, equivalent to east Semai *tei'*), which usually comprises the catchment basin of a particular river. The rights differ for the two categories of people. Those descended from the founders can hunt, fish, collect forest products, cultivate crops, and plant and own fruit and rubber trees in the village land. Residents who have married in have all the same rights except the right to own trees there, although they can plant trees on behalf of their spouses or children, who do have full rights. During fruit season, therefore, there is a lot of movement and truancy from school, as people go back to their home village to harvest their trees. People whose parents come from different villages potentially have full rights in both territories, though they must take an interest in a village's affairs, if not actually live there, in order to activate those rights.

Like east Semai, villagers can clear a field in any unused part of the village land and hold exclusive rights over the field as long as they get food from it. Abandoned fields revert to the community. Although ownership of swiddens is transitory, ownership of fruit and rubber trees is enduring and can be inherited or transferred by sale. Villagers claim exclusive rights over trees that they themselves have planted. A set of brothers and sisters may jointly hold a grove of trees inherited from their mother or father, if the parent has expressed a wish that they do so.

Rules governing access to land and trees vary from place to place. The rather formalized system just described developed in the Tapah area in the 1920s to eliminate recurring disputes over land. It still fulfills that purpose, despite increasing pressures on land due to development, dispossession by "relocation," and the continuing influx of outsiders. However, the Malaysian government only recognizes individual ownership of fruit and rubber trees. Semai customs regarding ownership and use of land, like those of all Orang Asli, have no standing in law (Dentan and Ong 1995; Gomes 1986).

The basic unit of production and consumption is the household, normally a nuclear family, but sometimes including a few other relatives. Each household is a cooperating organization of individuals who contribute to its work and share its products; each is economically autonomous in relation to other households. As among east Semai, members of different households work together at large-scale tasks like clearing fields, but in the west people calculate how much they help others and expect an equal amount of help in return. Occasionally people invite members of other households to help harvest a crop or some fruit, when the work is more than one household can do. The owners allow the helpers to keep what they harvest, but with an expectation that the recipients will reciprocate the favor in the future.

Because households are autonomous in making economic decisions, they differ in how much time they allocate to different economic activities. These decisions reflect personal preferences of household members and also the resources they have available, especially the number of fruit trees they own. Fruit-selling is the most lucrative activity available, and people normally spend as much time as it takes to market all the fruit their trees produce. All households keep a number of economic options in reserve, affording them some security in case one falls through. For example, if a family's fruit trees have a poor yield, they may collect forest products to sell to make up the difference. In several villages people have taken up novel enterprises like fish farming, oil palm and cocoa cultivation, and flower gardening to diversify their options.

One effect of household autonomy and a money economy is greater variation in household wealth than among east Semai. The most significant variation is in the number of fruit trees. This difference affects how much cash people can earn and thus whether they can buy expensive consumer goods, like motorcycles and television sets. Any resident can plant trees on village land, but trees take years to produce fruit and cash. Thus wealth in fruit trees stems more from the vagaries of inheritance than from a person's diligence.

Beginning in the 1920s, after the cessation of slave raids, west Semai began elaborating traditional agroforestry into planting fruit and rubber trees with an eye to selling the produce. As commercial tree crops became important, settlements became more permanent. Rather than moving their houses to be near their fields, they rotated their fields around their villages and associated orchards.

Today the two most profitable fruits produced are *petai* and *durian*. The *petai* tree is a legume which produces its seeds—which are made into a pungent, popular vegetable condiment—inside a huge pod, like a foot-long green bean. Harvesting *petai* requires climbing the tree and cutting the pods down before they dry and burst, scattering the seeds on the ground. Men usually do the climbing, but women and children may help tie up the bundles of pods and carry them home.

Durian is famous throughout Southeast Asia as a fruit with a foul odor—it has been likened to that of rotten onions—and a heavenly flavor. The fruit is the size and shape of a pineapple, armed with wicked-looking spikes on the surface. The large seeds inside are surrounded by creamy flesh, which tastes like a rich custard. Because *durian*s fall when ripe, both men and women collect them, but the heavy work of transporting them falls mainly to men. People carry all species of fruits out to the road, where they sell them to passersby or middlemen.

Rubber trees also provide some income. Men and women tappers go out early in the morning, cut a fresh groove at an oblique angle in the bark of each tree, and attach a small cup at the base of the groove to catch the latex. An hour later they return, collect the latex in a tin, and take it back to the village processing place where they coagulate it into slabs with formic acid. They feed the slabs through a manually operated rolling machine to squeeze out the water and produce a flat sheet of rubber. They hang the sheets to dry in the sun before selling them to rubber dealers.

Another source of cash is the sale of forest products—including rattan, bamboo, and insects—from the village's hinterland. Usually a few men go together to look for rattan, which is increasingly scarce, deep in the forest. The collector climbs the tree in which the rattan is lodged, cuts the vine loose from its crown, climbs down, and cuts the vine into nine-foot sections. He then ties the pieces into a bundle weighing as much as a hundred pounds and carries it on his shoulder to a spot where a middleman will pick it up. Men and women cut down bamboo, which is sold to Chinese vegetable farmers and basket-makers. It is usually abundant on the slopes near a village and can easily be dragged back. A small but steady income comes from collecting the exotic insects that Chinese middlemen frame and sell to tourists. During the day, men, women, and truant school children with homemade nets walk along forest streams in search of butterflies. At night they use powerful flashlights to hunt for huge leaf-insects, stick-insects, beetles, scorpions, and centipedes.

Another source of income is wage labor. A few west Semai are salaried—mainly in the JHEOA, army, and police—but most wage-earners are day laborers on non-Semai vegetable farms and tea plantations in the Cameron Highlands or at fruit plantations, rubber estates, and tin mines elsewhere. Payment for work done is not immediate, as it is in commodity selling. Employment is not steady. The attractiveness of the various cash-earning activities rises and falls as prices and wages change, and the relative advantages vary from place to place. People usually work at whichever activity is most lucrative at the time.

Although west Semai now buy most of their food, they still produce some themselves. In most years a few families clear and plant swiddens, like east Semai. But nowadays they seldom grow rice, as they find it cheaper in time and effort to buy it. Some communities no longer even have specialists who know how to perform the rituals for growing rice. The major swidden crops are tapioca and maize. Hunting, trapping, and fishing provide most animal protein in the west Semai diet. Besides blowpipe hunting, a few men use dogs and shotguns to kill bigger game, like pigs and deer.

West Semai, like their eastern counterparts, routinely share surplus food with families in nearby houses and sometimes share with other relatives and friends. A hunter who kills a large animal usually, though not always (see below), asks the headman to parcel out the meat to the whole village or at least a part of it. A family which has grown some rice will feast the village and other relatives at harvest time. Even so, food sharing is more restricted than in the east because there is less inter-family cooperation, and because families who buy food instead of producing it more accurately control how much food they have and thus have fewer surpluses. There is no obligation to share money, so one family can hoard its money even when another has no food. Buying food facilitates calculation in food sharing. People would stop sharing with a family that did not reciprocate in a timely fashion. Thus west Semai sharing tends toward "balanced reciprocity," in which people expect parity over time, instead of the "generalized reciprocity," uncalculated sharing, practiced by east Semai and Batek.

Perhaps the most striking difference between the east and west Semai is the great extent to which the west Semai economy is involved in market exchange. A detailed study of Semai families near Tapah in 1982-1984 (Gomes 1986, 1989) showed that families bought 88 percent or more of their food. They spent about three times as much time on money-earning work—commodity production and wage labor—as on subsistence. The pervasive desire to make money had transformed many social relations. People expected payment for helping relatives on projects like building houses, help that east Semai would give freely. Some families set up small shops in the village, though the businesses foundered on the conflict between commercial values—cash on the barrelhead—and traditional values of mutual assistance among kin, which led the shopkeepers' relatives to expect to be able to run up a tab. In their zeal to earn money, some hunters who killed large animals would take them not to their own village, where they would have to share the meat, but to another village, where they could sell it. This emphasis on earning money grows from two factors. One is that the west Semai, extensively exposed to markets and relatively affluent outsiders, have developed a taste for goods like motorbikes that only money can buy. The other is that, at prevailing prices, it is cheaper (in time and effort), as well as less risky, to buy staples like rice than to grow those foods themselves. The Tapah families satisfied their needs by working less than three hours per person per day. West Semai, in short, are simply making rational economic decisions in the context of the opportunities available to them. They have adapted to the market economy without help or pressure from the government.

Men and women share child care and domestic chores, though women do more than men. Men are responsible for building and maintaining houses, except for the thatch. Women do most of the firewood collecting, cooking, and washing. Men generally do the work which requires upper-body strength, like climbing trees and carrying rattan, or extended absences, like working on tea estates. They thus do much of the money-earning work, while women concentrate on subsistence and domestic activities. Yet women can be economically independent because they can get income from their trees, even if they do not do the work of tapping or collecting the fruit themselves, and from subsistence farming, which they can do anywhere in the village territory.

West Semai kinship reflects their peasant economy and the influence of their non-Semai neighbors. Consanguineal ties are narrower than among east Semai, limited to the descendants of one's great-grandparents. Marriages involve a Malay-style ceremony which confers clearly defined obligations on the couple and their relatives. As in the east, people generally chose their marriage partners themselves, with little interference from their relatives. Since consanguines cannot be partners, spouses normally come from different villages. Once a couple have agreed to marry, their parents meet and plan the wedding, exchanging tobacco and betel nut to symbolize their agreement. The families split the wedding expenses equally, calling on their consanguines and the residents of neighboring villages—who will all be wedding guests—for contributions. At the ceremony the couple sits together on a mat. An elder stands behind them and asks for a public blessing. Then the couple exchange cigarettes, which signifies that they are legally married. The groom's kinsmen present the bride's kinsmen with a gift of money—"brideprice"—and both parties make a small payment to the headman of the settlement where the wedding takes place. His acceptance of these gifts expresses his willingness to help make the marriage last. The next hour or so is taken up by elders lecturing the couple and the audience on their obligations toward this marriage. The groom's relatives must treat the wife well; if her mistreatment leads to divorce, they forfeit any claim to the return of the brideprice. The wife's relatives hear that the money is for emergencies, not frivolities. The main thrust of the orations is that each should turn to in-laws in times of trouble, rather than going home to their consanguines. The wedding ends with a feast for all the guests. The measures taken to involve both sets of relatives and their communities in the success of the marriage seem effective, for west Semai marriages are more durable than those of east Semai.

After the wedding the couple alternates residence between the bride's and groom's villages, as in the east, but here the motivation seems less to alleviate homesickness than to maintain control over the fruit trees that the couple own in their respective villages. Unlike east Semai, west Semai defer to all in-laws; sex between brothers- and sisters-in-law is not allowed. West Semai, like Malays, frown on sexual freedom, an attitude which emphasizes the sexual monopoly of marriage and the unity of the nuclear family.

The west Semai political system is more complex and formal than that of the east Semai. In 1909 the Sultan of Perak, through the local Malay chief, appointed Semai headmen for west Semai groups. Armed with royal letters of appointment and elaborate titles, they instituted a formal legal system and political structure modeled on Malay custom (*adat*). The regional headman conducted public meetings (*bicara'*, Malay for "trials") in the presence of the wrong-doer's kin, who could speak in his or her defense. Guilty offenders were fined. *Bicara'* functioned to defuse disputes between individuals, families, or villages. This system persists today (Robarchek 1977:214-22; 1979).

The newly titled leaders also organized the meeting of elders that formalized the existing system of village territories. The elders agreed that each village (band) should have a headman and one or more assistant headmen under the overall authority of the new leaders. For about a decade, beginning in the 1920s, the titled appointees annually collected fruit, mushrooms, hill rice, and forest products from Semai and presented part of the collection to local Malay chiefs as tribute, to placate the Malays. The rest of the produce went to feast their followers.

The Japanese invasion in 1941 and the subsequent Emergency (Communist insurrection) disrupted this west Semai political system. After the Emergency ended in 1960, the JHEOA took over as patron from the Sultan of Perak. Every Semai village still has a headman and at least one assistant headman who are responsible for all relations with outside authorities, resolving internal disputes, and coordinating village-wide activities. They are paid for their services and expenses by means of a small tax (*komisen*) levied on the sale of commodities to traders. Recently, however, some Semai have begun to refuse to pay the tax—or at least to pay it in full—claiming that the headmen merely use it to enrich themselves. Egalitarian values still seem to be undermining any tendency for the present political system to create a separate ruling class of the Malay sort.

In spite of the recent political stability in Malaysia, west Semai still see the world as threatening and unpredictable. This anxiety leads most of them to avoid conflict, especially violent conflict. But violence, often associated with alcohol, seems to be on the increase (see Chapter 5).

West Semai religion, like that of east Semai, involves warding off illness and misfortune by following prohibitions and using shamans who can enlist the aid of spirit familiars to find lost souls and combat dangerous spirits. Some west

Semai have become nominal Christians or Bahai as a defense against Malay pressures on them to become Muslims.

Many west Semai have integrated themselves into the Malaysian mainstream without government help. In principle, their way of life is the kind the Malaysian ruling class wants all Orang Asli to adopt, because it is settled, makes efficient use of land, and is integrated into the market economy. But the ruling class has failed to acknowledge the one right that west Semai need to keep their way of life viable—their right to the land on which they have lived for centuries and which they have made productive. Almost half a century after independence, Semai still lack secure land tenure. Consequently they are losing the resource base upon which their prosperity and independence depend.

TEMUAN: LOWLAND RICE FARMERS AND TRADERS (1978)[5]

With a population of over 10,000, the Temuan are one of the largest Orang Asli groups. They reside in small villages (between 50 and 500 people) in lowland valleys in Selangor and Negri Sembilan, with a few villages in Pahang and Malacca (see Map). Temuan are physically indistinguishable from Malays. They speak colloquial rural Malay, but with a few distinctive terms of their own and a slightly unusual accent.

The Temuan settlement of Kampung Paya Lebar in Ulu Langat, Selangor, about twenty-four miles from Kuala Lumpur, had a population of eighty-six in 1978. The village lay in a wide, marshy valley, about 300 feet above sea level, surrounded by steep, forested ridges rising to over 3,000 feet. It consisted of a cluster of small thatched houses, occupied by a group of closely related nuclear families.

Like west Semai, the Temuan of Paya Lebar were basically rural peasants. They grew some subsistence crops, hunted

---

5.   Alberto Gomes did fieldwork with Temuan in 1977-1979. For further information on Temuan, see Baharon 1973, 1986; Dunn 1975; Gomes 1982; Ali M.A. Rachman 1984, 1985; Ong Hean Chooi 1986.

and gathered in nearby forests, and fished in local streams. To get cash for food, cigarettes, clothing, and tools, they tapped rubber, collected forest products, sold fruit, and did occasional wage labor. They diverged from west Semai, however, in one significant respect: their main economic activity was cultivating irrigated rice.

The villagers grew rice mostly for their own consumption. In 1978 they planted about 14 acres, 0.7 acres per family, with three varieties of rice. Different families planted rice every year, every other year, or even twice a year. Cultivating wet rice takes a high input of energy in a number of related activities, including preparation of rice fields, weeding, engineering irrigation and drainage canals, guarding the ripening rice from pests, harvesting, threshing, winnowing, and drying.

As in other Temuan villages, both men and women planted rice seeds in compact nursery plots, usually in August or September. While waiting for the seeds to sprout, villagers hoed the main fields and constructed dikes and canals. After hoeing, people laboriously transplanted the rice plants to the prepared fields, usually in October or November. About a week later, they channeled water from the main river into the fields to provide essential nutrients to the growing rice. Irrigating rice demands engineering skills, especially in regulating the flow of water. Too much or too little hurts the growth of rice plants. Shortly before harvest time the people drained the water from the fields.

Throughout the rice growing process, people had to continuously guard the rice from rice birds, field rats, and insects. Every family member was involved in guarding the ripening rice in some way. It was common to see young children armed with sling shots shooting at the rice birds. During the rice harvest groups wielding sticks hunted rats in the fields.

The harvest normally occurred in April. As in planting, both men and women harvested, using sickles or small finger-knives (*tuai*). They then threshed the rice and put it on mats in the sun to dry. Later they stored it in large sacks for future consumption. Before cooking it, women pounded it with wooden pestles to remove the husk. The rice yields at

Paya Lebar were high relative to other rice growing areas. But most families did not get enough rice from their fields to meet their annual needs, so they had to buy some rice from shops in nearby Malay settlements.

The Temuan kinship system was similar to that of west Semai. Temuan also reckoned kinship ties through both parents. Because close relatives could not marry, spouses usually came from different villages, thus creating inter-village ties. In theory a young man's father would ask the village headman to find a suitable bride in another village. In practice, however, the choice of partners was left to the principals themselves. The Temuan wedding ceremony resembled the traditional Malay ceremony. It involved a wedding feast (*kenduri*) for relatives and friends of both families. The bride and groom sat side-by-side on a decorated "throne," like royalty. Their maternal uncles (*wali*) exchanged pouches containing betel nut, betel leaves, and lime paste. Then the couple fed each other with food served to them. Afterward, the groom's *wali* presented a small sum of money, the "bride price," to the bride's *wali*. The couple were then officially married.

Like other southern Orang Asli, Temuan have an elaborate village political hierarchy, with seven ranked leadership positions: *batin, pemangku, jekara, jenang, penghulu balai, menteri,* and *panglima*. The *batin* ("headman"), a male elder, has the most authority and prestige. In Paya Lebar he was the supreme advisor, the last court of appeal, and was respected for his magical powers. As a customary token of respect, villagers gave him a small share of their rice harvest and any large game obtained. A *batin* should have a strong personality, wide knowledge and experience, and an ability to be just and fair. After his death, his eldest son usually succeeds him. If the son is unqualified, however, the villagers choose someone else.

A *pemangku* assists the *batin* in administering the village, e.g., distributing meat obtained by hunters among village households. The *jenang* and *jekara* lead and supervise village cooperative work and take over the responsibility of village administration in the absence of the *batin* and *pemangku*. The *penghulu balai* ("head of the hall") manages and supervises village feasts and ceremonies. The *menteri* is like a "minister of foreign affairs," organizing relations with other villages. The *panglimas*, usually numbering four, were apparently village military leaders in the past. With the cessation of slave raids, their function has become obsolete.

This complex political system goes back many centuries among southern Orang Asli. It appears to be indigenous, not imposed by outsiders. It may represent a response to Mon or Malay colonialism and the need to organize external trade (Benjamin 1985).

While Temuans spoke of a high god called "Tuhan," they were basically animists. They believed that spirits, known as *hantu*, inhabit large boulders, rivers, tall trees, and mountains. Of the seven categories of *hantu*, only three were significant in daily life: ghosts, which could be either good or evil; bird spirits, dangerous and evil *hantu* usually taking the shape of ghastly creatures; and *hantu lidah tanah*, a *hantu* in animal form with one eye in the middle of its forehead and hands resembling the paws of a bear. People entering the forest took care to avoid encountering *hantu* and asked permission of *hantu* believed to inhabit an area before "trespassing." Like other Orang Asli, they attributed disease and sickness to *hantu*. Sick people normally consulted a herbalist or ritual specialist, who performed rituals and provided herbal remedies to fight off *hantu*.

Kampung Paya Lebar is no longer where it was in 1978. To expand their rice fields, Malays from the neighboring village gradually took over the best Temuan rice land by obtaining legal titles to it. To avoid confrontation and further harassment as the Malay population increased, the Temuan moved to another location in 1980. Since then they have been forced to move several times. They no longer plant irrigated rice. Contrary to the stereotypes of development planners, increasing contact with the "outside world" has caused the Paya Lebar Temuans, like some other Orang Asli groups, to change from sedentary rice farmers to nomads living in uncertainty.

3

Government Intervention

A History of Orang Asli Relations with the Outside World

> Boy who's black and uppity
> Nigger kid uncivilized
> Living on the upper river
> You like to eat macaques and langurs
> [Slurping] gallons of water at the waterhole
> Where frogs do their croaks at night.
>
> Malay aristocrat addressing a Malay mistaken for
> an Orang Asli in a Malay epic (Sturrock and Win-
> stedt 1957:71-72)[1]

At first glance they looked human, like us, but they were really like animals. Except, even animals know how to clean themselves. These didn't know how. Their hair was as matted as [the open weave on a] backbasket. It wasn't anything like the color of human hair. It was all splotchy with dirt and tree sap. It looked like tree bark. God only knows how many grubs and bugs were in it. And they didn't wear shirts or sarongs, not a thread of cloth, just

---

1.   Unless otherwise noted, all translations from Malay are by Dentan.

> *loincloths made out of jackfruit-tree barkcloth as wide as*
> *the palm of your hand. Their beards and mustaches were*
> *raggedy. Their whole lives long they'd never shaved or*
> *trimmed them. The skin of their bodies sometimes didn't*
> *look human but like layers of dirt soaked in tree sap. Glop*
> *from their eyes dibbled down their cheeks.*
>
> Late nineteenth century upper class Malay
> encountering Semai for first time (Abdullah
> 1960:277)

Before 1948

Until the government adopted the term "Orang Asli" in the 1960s, the aborigines of the Malay Peninsula were known in Malay as *Sakai*. The term *Sakai* may derive from Sanskrit *sakhi*, meaning "friend, companion, comrade" (Couillard 1984:85). By the end of the nineteenth century, the term meant "subordinate, slave, savage, aboriginal person." *Sakai* was (and is) as offensive to Orang Asli as "nigger" is to African-Americans and includes some of the same connotations of racial difference, inferiority, and powerlessness. The changing connotations of the term reflect the changing relations between Orang Asli and "outsiders" from the first millennium A.D. to the mid-twentieth century (Couillard 1984; Dentan i.p.).

By the middle of the first millennium A.D., Indian traders were going to the Malay Peninsula, followed by Indian-influenced traders from the Sumatran kingdom of Srivijaya between the seventh and thirteenth centuries (Andaya and Andaya 1982). They were seeking forest products like resins and rattan from the ancestors of the Orang Asli. They stopped at coastal or riverine villages or collection points and dealt with local middlemen or the collectors themselves (Dunn 1975:110-114). Probably these Hinduized traders called their trading partners—but not Orang Asli in general—*Sakai* (Couillard 1988:85-86). The original connotations of the term suggest that relations between local and foreign traders were not hierarchical or coercive. Probably the success of the foreign traders depended upon their ability to establish relations of trust with trade partners who could arrange the delivery of the desired forest products.

As trade grew, some of the more important ports, notably Malacca on the west coast of the Peninsula, developed into the seats of small, Indian-style kingdoms. Malaccan society included a ruling class, headed by a royal family from Sumatra; their followers, servants, and retainers, including a "navy" composed of "Sea People" (*Orang Laut*); an international community of resident traders; and a large population of commoners in the surrounding hinterland. Almost all the hinterland commoners were Orang Asli, and those on the coast were Orang Laut—Austronesian-speaking fishermen, traders, and pirates (Andaya and Andaya 1982:12, 45-50). The rulers incorporated Orang Asli leaders—called *batin*, as among Temuan today—as low-level functionaries responsible for managing trade in forest products. Commoners owed the ruler military service and corvée labor. In Malay epics about Malacca the term *Sakai* refers to commoners summoned to perform a job, for example, as crew members on a royal voyage (Couillard 1984:89). Thus it meant something like "subjects liable to corvée labor."

After the rulers of Malacca became Muslim in the early fifteenth century, Islam slowly spread to the general populace, dividing those indigenous people who rejected Islam and retained some independence from those who accepted it and became more integrated into the state. The former remained Orang Asli, while the latter became Malays. Records from the nearby Jelai area show how this was expressed politically. Converts moved from the direct authority of the aboriginal headman (*batin*) to that of the territorial headman (*penghulu*), a state official, but one who received his office from the *batin* (Hooker 1976:179; Couillard 1984:90-91). Thus those people who maintained their aboriginal religions remained outside the direct control of Malay colonialism.

Accelerating immigration of Austronesians from the islands of modern-day Indonesia accompanied and stimulated the growth of kingdoms in the Peninsula. Some earlier immigrants respected the prior rights of the indigenous Orang Asli. For example, matrilineal Minangkabau settlers from Sumatra, who later made up the bulk of the population of the state of Negri Sembilan, married Orang Asli women to establish rights to land through the female line. In the early days,

Orang Asli *batin* had "the power of electing the Malay chiefs" (Newbold 1839:392) and took part in the "installation of every new Raja" (Logan 1847:327). In the legendary history of the northern state of Perak, the founder of the Malay kingdom, Nakhodah Kasim, married a Semang girl (Maxwell 1882). But she was a supernatural personage, with white blood and a miraculous birth from a bamboo plant. Thus the story side-steps any implication that the Perak dynasty descends from an Orang Asli, although Semai still recount their version of this story (Juli 1990:48-50; Dentan i.p.). By the mid-nineteenth century, however, Orang Asli no longer played any part in Malay politics (Favre 1848:270), and Malays forgot their myths of the Orang Asli role in the founding of the Malay kingdoms.

European intervention beginning in the sixteenth century caused political turmoil throughout Island Southeast Asia. In 1511 Portuguese invaders captured Malacca. They in turn lost it to the Dutch in 1641. Finally the British gained control of Malacca in 1795, in the wake of the Napoleonic wars (Andaya and Andaya 1982). The turmoil greatly affected the Malay Peninsula.

> The conflict arising in the different parts of the Archipelago resulted in important migrations towards the Peninsula where Minangkabau, Bugis, Javanese and other pioneers moved up rivers and settled in the valleys. These settlers came into open conflict with the Orang Asli for access to land. Some of them imposed themselves violently, others opted for alliances, especially matrimonial, legitimising in the process their moving into Orang Asli territories. During this period the demand for tin increased and tin mines multiplied. Malay chiefs called upon immigrants to work in these mines. . . . The trade of forest products also bloomed, but in the nineteenth century the Orang Asli were not alone in collecting these products. The settlers who opened up the forest increasingly participated in this trade side by side with the Orang Asli and in direct competition

with them for access to the territory. (Couillard 1984:99, citing Dunn 1975:18)

Relations between Orang Asli and local Malays also deteriorated in the eighteenth century as Malay chiefs and headmen tried to tighten their control over Orang Asli collectors of forest products (Couillard 1984:100).

Enslaving Orang Asli is an ancient tradition in the Peninsula, going back before the arrival of Pasisir (aristocratic Malaccan) culture and perhaps before the arrival of the Malays themselves. Semai still tell stories about pre-Malay times, when "Jknvng" slavers from northeast Pahang raided them. Perhaps these were colonists from the ancient Mon kingdoms to the north who exploited gold and tin deposits in northern Pahang. Semai say they spoke a language like their own (Austroasiatic?) and wore bronze fishhooks (chainmail brassarts?) on their arms.

Slavery was long established in the Indianized kingdoms of Island Southeast Asia as well. In that hierarchical social world the raja had absolute power over all his subjects, and members of different social classes were bound together by personalized patron-client ties in which those above had the rights and those below the obligations. There were even two ranks of slaves, "debt slaves" (*orang berhutang*), who lost their freedom by being unable to repay a debt, being above "bought slaves" (*abdi*). In theory debt slaves—usually Malays in the Malay kingdoms—were freemen with some rights, while bought slaves had none. Owners could neglect, abuse, or even kill the latter at will. Because Islam forbids enslaving Muslims, the vast majority of bought slaves circulating in the slave markets were pagans captured in the Philippines and the islands of modern Indonesia. In the Peninsula the logical candidates for capture were the Orang Asli, indigenes who had not adopted Islam (Endicott 1983).

Immigrant "Malays," having no stake in the forest product trade with the Orang Asli, therefore raided them for slaves, who could easily be sold in slave markets. Orang Asli tend to blame "Indonesian Malays" rather than "indigenous Malays" for the raids that occurred in the last century or two. Under British rule, the intensification of tin mining, wet-rice agriculture, and plantation arboriculture (tree crops) made owning slaves more profitable. It also attracted Indonesians and Muslim Indian adventurers looking to make a quick profit. Javanese settled thickly in Selangor, displacing Btsisi' who had fled there from the south. Orang Rawa from Sumatra moved into south Perak, establishing bases from which in the latter part of the nineteenth century they launched a sustained campaign against Orang Asli, forcing Jah Hut to seek refuge in southern Pahang. Semai and Jah Hut still tell stories of the "Sangkil War" with the Rawas; for, although they could not resist the superior technology of the slave raiders, they could wage a successful guerrilla campaign against would-be occupiers.

Revisionist historians (Dodge 1981; Sullivan 1982) have argued that slavery in Malaysia was a relatively benign institution, just one variation on the "relations of dependency" that pervaded feudal Malay society. For example, household slaves were supposedly treated like members of the family, albeit ones who performed the duties of servants and could be punished at will. The revisionists claim that the British exaggerated the brutality of slavery as a pretext for extending their control over Peninsular kingdoms in the nineteenth century.

Whatever the living conditions of slaves were—and reports suggest that they varied widely—the method by which they were obtained was far from humane (Endicott 1983:221-224). All Orang Asli recall stories of slave raids told to them by their parents and grandparents; a few people still, as of this writing, remember raids personally. The raiders ambushed isolated homesteads, killing all the men past puberty they could catch. They gang-raped the women and then dragged them along to be raped again before they were killed. Children under the age of ten or twelve were small enough to transport easily over the difficult mountain terrain and—having seen their relatives brutalized and butchered—could be "tamed" (Malay *memperjinak*) more easily than adults, who might still have wanted to escape. Some Orang Asli were complicitous in these raids. For example, Temiar seem to have been willing to lead raiders to Semai settlements or to kidnap children, in part to escape being raided themselves.

Orang Asli still spend a lot of energy trying to make children aware of the dangers of being snatched or ripped apart by outsiders. Orang Asli women still profess to be afraid to leave their settlements for fear that Malays will kidnap or rape them. Centuries of slaving have made Orang Asli cautious and prone to retreat from situations which could escalate into violence.

It may seem difficult to understand how Malays could have demonstrated an inhuman insensitivity and brutality toward Orang Asli which is wholly at odds with their ordinary behavior. The picture becomes clearer if one understands that there were no social or moral ties between Malays and free Orang Asli. To Malays, Orang Asli were jural nonpersons, living outside the web of ethical, political, and moral ties which bind people together and govern their behavior (Andaya and Andaya 1982:160-161). Ethical constraints were no more relevant than they would have been in an encounter with a stray dog. One could be kind to it or feed it, beat it or kill it, without compunction. Some Malays, particularly those indigenous to the area, lived in peace as neighbors of Orang Asli, choosing to recognize them as human neighbors. Others killed and enslaved them, choosing to recognize them as wild beasts. For instance, when a high official of the state of Kedah sent a couple of Semang slaves to some British friends in Penang for their amusement, one of the Semang, never having been in a boat, panicked. Rather than risk swamping the boat, the Malays killed him and threw him overboard (Anderson 1824:xli). No one involved seems to have thought a murder had occurred.

By the end of the eighteenth century the Orang Asli had withdrawn inland to escape predation and were no longer the valued "dependents" and traders they had once been. Couillard (1984:101) believes that it was between the sixteenth and nineteenth centuries that

> the term *sakai* acquired a negative connotation. It probably referred then either to Orang Asli who fled inland, refusing integration and reverting to a tribal

way of life, or to those who were the victims of the
hunt for slaves. *Sakai* in this context came to refer to
the lowest social group in the Peninsula.

She adds, insightfully, that it was in this marginalized
condition that "they came within the purview of the nascent
field of anthropology, that they were redefined as 'savage'
(the 'wild men' of Skeat and Blagden) and protected as an en-
dangered 'species'" (1984:102).

In the nineteenth century the British began to push their
control beyond their crown colonies of Penang, Malacca, and
Singapore into the Malay states of the Peninsula. British policies and attitudes did not help Orang Asli. As mentioned,
British economic endeavors attracted numerous Indonesian
(and Chinese) immigrants and also increased the demand for
slaves. The political strategy of "indirect rule," which left the
sultans in charge of Malay customs and religion, "reinforced
the distinction between Muslims and non-Muslims and thus
isolated further the Orang Asli" (Couillard 1984:101). "The
introduction of titles and the appropriation by the state of all
non-cultivated land deprived the Orang Asli of free access to
land and pushed them into the least fertile regions" (Couillard 1984:102), marginalizing them still further. British officials were reluctant to oppose slavery, in part because they
knew it would sour relations with the Malay ruling class. "In
the Malay world the human resources represented by slaves
were as important to the status of a ruler or chief as revenue
itself" (Andaya and Andaya 1982:160). Many British administrators, being upper class and socialized in elite "public"
schools, felt an affinity with the Malay ruling class. For instance, both groups esteemed public piety, refined speech,
and good manners. The British called Malay aristocrats
"Asia's gentlemen." This feeling of affinity made them con-
done policies they might otherwise have found ethically troublesome.

However, in 1883, under pressure from abolitionist organizations in England, the British finally acquired enough re-
solve to abolish slavery in the populous state of Perak. By
1920 it was officially abolished in all states under British control, though it persisted in disguised form. As the danger of

slave raids declined, trade in forest products revived. Malay middlemen attempted to control the terms of trade by establishing patron-client relationships with their Orang Asli partners (e.g., getting them into debt) and by enforcing monopolies against rival middlemen. Europeans and Americans tend to think of trade as entirely different from slavery. Traditional Southeast Asians did not make this distinction in a clear-cut way. Consider, for example, the relationship Schebesta (1928:32-33) found in 1924 between Semang foragers and their Malay trade partners.

> All over the peninsula the Semang . . . live in a state of more or less dependence upon the Malays. Whenever I encountered a group, I discovered that they had made some sort of pact with a Malay. To him they brought from time to time the products of the forest, which they exchanged for rice, iron knives, or cloth. The Malay in this way exercises a certain degree of protectorship in regard to the forest dwarfs, whom, it goes without saying, he does not always treat honourably, and so often reaps great personal profit from this arrangement. If he requires them to work for him, he fetches them out of the forest and often rewards them most inadequately for their hard labour. More than once they came to me in trouble and showed me the handful of rice with which the Malay had paid them for a day's work. The men and women complained bitterly of the extortionate methods of their masters. Of course the Semang today [several decades after the British colonial government outlawed slavery] are not compelled to leave the forest in order to work for the Malays, but hunger and the craving to eat rice at least once a month drives them out.

Discounting Schebesta's paternalism and consequent anti-Malay bias, one sees a system which mixes elements of slavery, clientage, and trade. Orang Asli in this way were admitted to the margins of Malay society geographically and to its lowest rank socially. But, except during the trade itself, they remained nonpersons to their Malay "patron," who might threaten to murder or enslave them if they failed to produce.

Between the turn of the century and World War II, the colonial government treated Orang Asli with benign neglect, attending to them only when they broke game or forestry laws. The state of Perak was the exception. In 1901 state officials offered Captain G. B. Cerruti, an Italian adventurer with a romantic interest in Orang Asli, a post as "Superintendent of the Sakais." He spent sixteen years getting to know west Semai and Temiar and attempting to help them with their problems. He wrote an engaging memoir and ethnographic summary whose title, *My Friends the Savages* (1908), neatly summarizes sympathetic Europeans' views of Orang Asli at the time. Some administrators, like W. W. Skeat, were part-time scholars who made valuable studies of Orang Asli and Malays. I. H. N. Evans, the Director of the Perak Museum in Taiping between 1913 and 1932, made the Museum a center of research on Orang Asli. In 1931 a young anthropology graduate from Cambridge University, H. D. ("Pat") Noone joined the Museum as field ethnographer. He began a lifelong love affair with the Temiar, taking a Temiar wife and publishing a scholarly monograph on Temiar life (Noone 1936). In 1939 he drafted the first formal government policy on Orang Asli, the Aboriginal Tribes Enactment—Perak: No. 3, which was to become a basis for later government policies (Holman 1958:66). Among other things it recommended that the government establish aboriginal reservations and a Protector of Aborigines. Noone himself was duly appointed to that position.

In December 1941 the Japanese invaded the Peninsula and occupied it until 1945. During that period most Orang Asli retreated into the forest and avoided contact with the outside world. They shared the forest with the Malayan Peoples Anti-Japanese Army (MPAJA), a Communist-dominated guerrilla force that formed the only effective resistance to the Japanese occupiers. The MPAJA, mostly Chinese, received support from Chinese squatters and villagers, whom the Japanese treated cruelly. A few British soldiers, who went underground after the invasion, worked with the MPAJA and gave them military training (Chapman 1957). The guerrillas lived in clandestine camps and carried out sabotage and terrorist attacks against Japanese outposts and those they considered collaborators, especially police.

> Members of the M.P.A.J.A. carefully nurtured
> friendships with the Orang Asli and it seems that
> they even went as far as to protect the jungle peoples
> from the attacks of bandits and Japanese troops. In
> return the Orang Asli aided the Communist forces
> by providing porters, guides, food and intelligence
> on Japanese movements if the latter should venture
> into deep jungle. (Jones 1968:294)

The guerrillas generally treated Orang Asli with respect and
won their cooperation, if not support for their cause.

The Emergency (1948-1960)[2]

After the Japanese surrender in August 1945, the British
returned to Malaya to reestablish colonial rule. Communist
leaders, hoping to play a dominant role in a post-indepen-
dence government, initially cooperated, but soon realized
they could not achieve their goals legally. In 1947 the Communists returned to armed struggle. In June 1948 guerrillas
began ambushing police and European managers of rubber
plantations. Thus began the "Emergency," the Communist
insurgency that officially lasted from 1948 to 1960.

In an effort to cut off the guerrillas from their rural supporters, the British resettled 500,000 mostly Chinese squatters
in guarded settlements called "new villages." "Resettlement,
combined with the intensification of military activity by the
Security Forces, forced the Communist insurgents to retreat
to the deep jungle where long established friendships with
Orang Asli were renewed" (Jones 1968:295).

The insurgents organized Orang Asli and guerrillas in
each river basin in the mountainous interior into *asal* commit-
tees. (*Asal* is a variant of *asli*, meaning "original," "aboriginal.") "The choice of this word was clever, for at that time
both the government and the population in general were still
referring to the aborigines as 'sakai,' a derogatory term meaning 'slave'" (Carey 1976:310). Each *asal* committee consisted of

---

2.   For further information on Orang Asli during the Emergency, see
     Jones 1968; Carey 1976:290-295, 305-320; Dentan 1968:3, 80-81 and
     1995; Andaya and Andaya 1982:251-261; Leary 1995).

a prominent headman, as chairman, and a number of young Orang Asli, with a few insurgents as advisors. Nominally independent, they actually operated under the direction of Chinese guerrilla leaders.

> These asal groups were assigned a number of tasks. The most important of these was the provision of food and shelter for the terrorists. . . . In addition, the asal committees ensured a steady supply of guides and porters, and the population in general was directed to obtain information about troop movements and similar matters. Furthermore, selected Orang Asli were armed and asked to help the terrorists in their struggle more actively. Finally, it was the task of the asal groups to ensure that all the surrounding Orang Asli villages and settlements were under their effective control, and that they remained sympathetic to the cause of the terrorists. (Carey 1976:311)

In an effort to deny their support to the guerrillas, military authorities decided to resettle Orang Asli outside the forest. Their procedures showed incredible ignorance and callousness.

> A majority of the people concerned were brutally rounded up by the military or the police, put into trucks without any explanation, and transported in long convoys to the various centres of resettlement. Prior to their departure, the Orang Asli watched the destruction of their houses and the killing of their livestock. Thus they found themselves suddenly surrounded by barbed wire, guarded day and night, and without proper shelter. Unlike the Chinese new villages, those which were established hastily for the Orang Asli resembled miniature concentration camps, although there was no overt cruelty—just ignorance and stupidity. It was apparent that some of the officers who had organized this type of resettlement were not fully aware of the fact that the Orang Asli, like other races, had the same needs for shelter and food. Instead, they regarded them in the same

manner as the wild animals in the jungle, and
thought that they would survive without further
help. (Carey 1976:307)

Resettlement was disastrous both for Orang Asli and for
the government's campaign to separate Orang Asli from the
insurgents. Lack of shelter, poor nutrition, unsanitary conditions, and total social and psychological upheaval killed
many resettled Orang Asli (Carey 1976:308; Jones 1968:297).
For example, "in 1951 it was reported that the death rate in
one large camp reached the figure of 204 per thousand which
it was feared would lead to the complete elimination of the
group concerned" (Jones 1968:297). Hundreds of Orang Asli
fled the camps and returned to their people, bringing horrify-
ing tales of their experience. Many who had not yet been resettled

> abandoned their villages and moved further into the
> deep jungle so as to avoid resettlement. There they
> sought the protection of the terrorists, and decided
> to collaborate with them more closely than they had
> ever done before. In short, the ill-considered and ill-
> advised policy of resettlement had exactly the oppo-
> site effect to what had been intended: the Orang Asli
> now supported the insurgents more actively and
> wholeheartedly than ever before. (Carey 1976:308)

By 1953 probably the entire Orang Asli population of the central highlands between the Negri Sembilan border and Thailand, upwards of 30,000 people (mostly east Semai and
Temiar), was under effective Communist control (Carey
1976:305, 311; Jones 1968:297).

When it became clear that resettlement had failed, the security forces adopted another approach. First they let the "de-
tainees" return to their home areas. Then they established
"jungle forts" in Orang Asli areas with high concentrations of
guerrillas. There were five jungle forts by 1954 and the number soon increased to ten (Carey 1976:312; Jones 1968:298).
The aim was to provide visible evidence of government authority and to protect Orang Asli from intimidation. "Forts
were garrisoned by members of Police Field Forces numbering approximately 35 to a Fort" (Jones 1968:298). Patrols reg-

ularly visited Orang Asli settlements in the vicinity of the forts. The police also armed some Orang Asli with shotguns and told them to defend themselves. At first Orang Asli feared the police and avoided the forts (Carey 1976:312). Later the police made the forts more attractive by offering basic medical care and opening small shops selling such goods as salt, tobacco, and metal tools (Carey 1976:313-314). But most Orang Asli did not live near forts, and the guerrillas came and went freely whenever the police were not around.

The resettlement fiasco and the limited success of jungle forts finally convinced the British to try winning over Orang Asli by kindness rather than coercion. The job fell primarily to the nascent Department of Aboriginal Affairs. In 1950 the government had appointed Major Peter D. R. Williams-Hunt the first Federal Advisor on Aborigines (Jones 1968:295). The position was purely advisory, however, and had no power. Williams-Hunt fell in love with Semai, as Noone did with Temiar, and he took a Semai woman, Wa' Draman, as his wife.[3] He published a short, charming book on Orang Asli for use by British bureaucrats and soldiers (Williams-Hunt 1952). Semai still regard his death in an accident the following year as one of the great tragedies of their history, in which he is a folk hero named Bah Janggut, "Mr. Beard," who protects and looks after his people. Williams-Hunt was succeeded by Richard O. D. Noone, the younger brother of Pat Noone and also a trained anthropologist.

In 1954, the government dramatically expanded the Department of Aboriginal Affairs and gave it new responsibilities (Jones 1968:299-300; Carey 1976:312-314). The Department posted one or two field assistants, mostly Malays with some police or military experience, and a couple of Orang Asli field staff at each jungle fort. Their job was to advise the police on how best to handle Orang Asli. They visited Orang Asli near the forts regularly to learn about the people's concerns and to gather intelligence on guerrilla activities. They also took over the education of Orang Asli children— teaching them to read and write Malay—which had been ini-

---

3. For an account of Williams-Hunt's life in Malaya, see Gouldsbury 1960.

tiated informally by police at the forts. The Department also posted male nurses at the forts to treat Orang Asli, and a doctor visited each fort about once a month. Seriously ill patients were flown out to hospital from the forts' airstrips. The Department also managed the small shops at the forts. These attractions proved popular and contributed to softening Orang Asli fear of the government.

Orang Asli tried to cope with the conflicting demands of the guerrillas and the government security forces in their own way. Wanting only to be left alone and allowed to live in peace, they tried to placate both groups. Some Temiar leaders devised an ingenious scheme to this end, and Semai quickly followed suit.

> The six points of the program were the following: (1) Bands upstream and thus near the Communists were to aver that they supported the Communists. (2) Bands down river in contact with the government forces were to "support" the government. (3) The "pro-Communist" and "pro-government" bands were to keep each other informed of the plans of *mai* ["outsiders"]. (4) The majority of the people, who were between these two groups, were to play dumb, which the Semai do superbly. . . . (5) No information was to be given *mai* that might endanger any Semai or lead to a battle for which the Semai might be blamed. (6) In the event of a Communist victory, the "pro-Communist" bands were to cover up for all the bands downstream from them, claiming that all had been pro-Communist. Conversely, if the government won, the "pro-government" bands were to cover for the bands upstream. (Dentan 1968:80-81)

Accordingly, as the tide of the conflict shifted in favor of the government, the number of Orang Asli supporting the guerrillas dwindled. "R. O. D. Noone estimated that there were only about 250 'hostile aborigines' in the whole of Malaya by mid 1958" (Jones 1968:300).

In the late 1950s the security forces formed an anti-guerrilla military unit composed mostly of Orang Asli, called the Senoi Praak or "Fighting Aborigines" (Jones 1968:300-301;

Carey 1976:317-318). Most recruits had formerly been armed supporters of the insurgents, but changed sides when the government began to get the upper hand. They were led initially by British and Malay officers, trained by the Special Air Service, and armed with modern weapons. They were already expert at living in the forest for extended periods. The Senoi Praak was a success. Members were especially good at tracking and liaising with local Orang Asli. The Senoi Praak has continued to the present as a small section of the Police Field Force specializing in deep forest duties.

By the late 1950s the government had the insurgency under control. The Federation of Malaya (independent since 1957) declared the Emergency officially over on July 31, 1960. But a few guerrillas remained at large until 1989, when the last stragglers surrendered. During the intervening years, the military strictly controlled access to the north central mountain range, home to east Semai, Temiar, Jahai, and Mendriq. Thus those groups eluded the full force of development until the late 1980s.

After 1960

Opening Parliament in 1961, the King declared that the nation would not forget the Orang Asli just because the Emergency was over. He said:

> My government is . . . engaged in evolving a long-term policy for the administration and advancement of the aborigines. . . . The ultimate objective must be to absorb these people into the stream of national life in a way, and at a pace, which will adopt and not destroy their traditional way of living and culture. (Quoted in Jones 1968:302)

The Ministry of the Interior issued a *Statement of Policy Regarding the Administration of the Aborigine Peoples of the Federation of Malaya* (Ministry of the Interior 1961) which details the government's policies regarding Orang Asli. The *Statement of Policy*, which reflects the King's concern for the integrity of Orang Asli cultures, lacks the force of law, however. As we will show, current government policy toward Orang

Asli ignores or directly contradicts many of its provisions (Mohd Tap 1990:45-46, 450).

In November 1961 the Department of Aboriginal Affairs (JHEOA) became permanent and totally responsible for administering the Orang Asli. One reason the government chose the single agency approach was that over 60 percent of Orang Asli still lived in isolated areas, distant from normal government services like education and medical care. The JHEOA staff had also developed expertise in dealing with Orang Asli. Security remained a major concern. Officials feared that even Orang Asli outside the restricted area might be susceptible to Communist propaganda. Therefore the Department was placed under the Ministry of the Interior (later renamed Ministry of Home Affairs), which is responsible for internal security. In 1966 the government officially adopted the term "Orang Asli" in place of English "Aborigines" and Malay *Sakai*. Officials hoped the new term would cause the public to view Orang Asli with more respect than they had in the past.

THE LEGAL POSITION OF THE ORANG ASLI TODAY[4]

> *The Orang Asli clearly occupy a unique and disadvantaged status in Malaysian society. Despite being an indigenous people they are not accorded any of the binding special privileges that are provided in the Constitution to the other indigenous people—the Malays, and the native peoples of Sabah and Sarawak.*
>
> S. Sothi Rachagan (1990:110)

---

4.   This section draws upon the following sources: the Federal Constitution of Malaysia (Malaysian Government 1982); the Aboriginal Peoples Act, 1954 (Malaysian Government 1994); Means 1985-1986; Tan Chee-Beng 1987; Rachagan 1990; Hooker 1976, 1991; Legal Correspondent 1991; Nicholas 1991a.

The Srigala Incident[5]

At the urging of a Christian missionary and using funds he supplied, the thirty Christians in the forty-person Semai settlement of Teiw Srigala' (Malay *Sungai Srigala*) in Selangor began in August, 1990, to build a M$16,000 church, which was also to serve as a kindergarten. On orders from the Malay District Officer, they applied for a building permit on September 2. On September 14 the D.O. denied their application on grounds that "certain" relevant laws forbade it.[6] The D.O. circulated several copies of this letter, including one to the Selangor Department of Religious Affairs.

The Semai unsuccessfully appealed the decision. The D.O. ordered them to destroy the building and accused the Christians, particularly their leader Bah Supeh, of illegally occupying government land. But Bah Supeh remained defiant:

> Why do we need to ask permission for? This is our land. Our people were here even before Tanjung Malim was opened. Horse-carts were still being used then. We've built our houses here, and cultivated rubber for generations. It makes no sense now telling us that we are occupying the land illegally. (Quoted in LKW/CN 1990:9)

Five days later the Semai dedicated their church.

On November 27, officials from the District Office, armed policemen, and Federal Reservists armed with batons, machetes, and M-16s invaded Teiw Srigala'. With the help of two bulldozers from the Public Works Department (JKR), they leveled the church. Everyone was taken aback. A Malay neighbor said, "This is a house of God. Why did they do this?" (LKW/CN 1990:10).

---

5.   This account draws on LKW/C[olin]N[icholas] 1990, Chan Looi Tat 1991, Loh 1993, and Dentan's personal observations in mid 1991.

6.   The word "certain" in official pronouncements conveys the connotation that specifying exactly what one is talking about will cause a lot of trouble, particularly for the people being directly or indirectly addressed. This usage is part of Malay periphrasis, which allows people to talk without confrontation.

JHEOA headquarters, recognizing the move as an overreaction on the D.O.'s part, moved swiftly to placate the people of Srigala. By January 1992 the settlement had a permanent kindergarten building, ten small windowless houses, and seven standpipes to supply clean water. But the Department did not replace the church.

The government clamped a news blackout on the story. Reporters from *Asiaweek*, a Hong Kong-based newsmagazine, visited Teiw Srigala' and did a photo-essay (Chan Looi Tat 1991). In the story Jimin Idris, then Director-General of the JHEOA, maintained carefully that the destruction of the church "was not legally wrong," because the law forbade erecting permanent buildings on "land which belongs to the state," as all Orang Asli land legally does. That issue of *Asiaweek* did not appear in Malaysia.

Without breaking the news blackout, the Orang Asli Association (POASM) took the JHEOA to court on the grounds that, if the JHEOA could erect a permanent community center and kindergarten on the land, then Semai could erect any sort of permanent building they chose. The JHEOA made two attempts to settle out of court that year. No one mentioned Section 295 of the Penal Code, which provides that anyone who "destroys, damages or defiles any place of worship . . . shall be punished with imprisonment for a term which may extend to two years, or with fine, or both."

This incident illustrates some of the serious legal and practical problems facing Orang Asli today. These include violations of their constitutionally guaranteed personal rights by government agencies, lack of rights over the land they live on, and weak support from the agency charged with protecting their rights, the JHEOA.

The Aboriginal Peoples Act

In 1954, when the Emergency was at its most critical stage, the colonial government enacted the "Aboriginal Peoples Act, 1954" (Malaysian Government 1994), which defines the legal position of Orang Asli. The British viewed Orang Asli mainly as innocent victims to be protected from the evil influence of the Communists. Therefore the Act gave the government extensive control over Orang Asli, in the interest of national security. The tone of the legislation is paternalistic, with the government in the position of parent to the Orang Asli children. This Act—with minor amendments in 1956, 1958, and 1967—is still in force today. It, together with the Federal Constitution and Malaysian land laws, still defines their legal rights and restrictions. We return below to the question of why Orang Asli should still be administered under laws enacted during a state of emergency thirty-five years after the emergency ended.

Personal Rights

The Federal Constitution (Malaysian Government 1982) recognizes Orang Asli as citizens, who, in theory, are guaranteed the same rights as all other citizens. These rights include equal treatment before the law, equal access to public education, equal right to own property, freedom of speech and peaceful assembly, and freedom to form associations. On the matter of religion, which is central to Orang Asli identity and an issue in the Srigala incident, the Constitution says that "Islam is the religion of the Federation; but other religions may be practiced in peace and harmony in any part of the Federation" (Article 3[1]). All Malaysians have the right to profess and practice their religions and to propagate them, except among Malays (Articles 11[1] and 11[4]). No one can be "required to receive instruction in or to take part in any ceremony or act of worship of a religion other than his own" (Article 12[3]). The Constitution (Article 12[4]) and the Aboriginal Peoples Act (Section 17[2]) guarantee that Orang Asli children under age eighteen will not be subjected to religious training without their parents' or guardians' prior consent. The Constitution also instructs the King to appoint at least one senator "capable of representing the interests of aborigines" (Article 45[2]) and authorizes special laws concerning them, meaning the "Aboriginal Peoples Act, 1954" (Article 8[5][c]).

The Aboriginal Peoples Act, however, takes away from Orang Asli a number of the normal rights and freedoms of citizens, originally in the interest of national security. The

Minister (of the Ministry responsible for Orang Asli welfare), his representative, or any police officer may prohibit any person or class of persons from entering any aboriginal area, aboriginal reserve, or aboriginally inhabited place, even if the person is invited by the Orang Asli (Sections 14 and 15). Similarly, the Minister may prohibit entry into Orang Asli communities of any written, printed, or photographic matter he deems harmful (Section 19[1][l]). He or she must confirm a group's choice of "headman" and can dismiss any headman from office (Section 16). The Minister may regulate what crops the people grow, what land they clear, what animals they hunt, and what jobs they take (Section 19). He or she can also exclude alcoholic beverages from Orang Asli communities (Section 19[1][m]). In addition no Orang Asli may make any land transaction without the consent of the Commissioner (Director-General) (Section 9), and the Commissioner must also approve any adoption of an Orang Asli child by non-Orang Asli (Section 18). "There is . . . no provision to allow the Orang Asli any role in the determination of their own affairs" (Rachagan 1990:110).

Given how extensive governmental control over Orang Asli is, it is not surprising that government officials, the Malaysian public, and Orang Asli themselves have come to believe that Orang Asli cannot do anything without the guidance and permission of the JHEOA. Generally speaking, any individual, company, or government agency wanting to do anything that affects Orang Asli must negotiate with the JHEOA rather than with the people concerned (Todd 1990:12). Department officials even tell Orang Asli how to vote, and for many years they dutifully delivered their support to the ruling UMNO party. There was much consternation in UMNO and the JHEOA in 1990, therefore, when rebellious Temiar in Kelantan threw their support to the leader of the opposition Semangat '46 party. In the early 1970s an American biologist who wanted to take a Temuan colleague to the U.S. for several months to finish a research project discovered that the Temuan man had to have the support of the JHEOA to get an international passport. Only after the biologist said she had no intention of converting her Temuan friend to Christianity did the Department give its approval.

No one asked why an adult Malaysian citizen could not get a passport or choose his religion without the permission of a government department.

The only special rights Orang Asli have, beyond those of other citizens, are qualified rights to hunt protected game and collect forest products for their own consumption when living in game or forest reserves. They do not have the privileged access to places in educational institutions, scholarships, jobs in the public service, or commercial licenses, which the Constitution guarantees to Malays and Borneo natives (Malaysian Federal Constitution, Article 153) (Rachagan 1990:110). Article 8(5)(c) of the Constitution *allows* the government to reserve positions in the public service for Orang Asli, but the government has not actually enacted such legislation. The "special privileges" of Malays were put into the original Constitution when the Federation of Malaya became independent in 1957 as part of the "Bargain" between the Malays, Chinese, and Indians. After the Federation expanded in 1963 to include Singapore, Sabah, and Sarawak—creating the Federation of Malaysia—the special privileges were extended to the natives of Sabah and Sarawak on the principle that they too are "indigenous" peoples. The ruling coalition has a large enough majority to amend the Constitution at any time, yet it has never added Orang Asli to the list of privileged groups, despite considerable agitation by Orang Asli and their supporters. The omission of Orang Asli from the privileged category is apparently not, then, a mere oversight, but is part of deliberate, albeit covert, government policy.

The fact that Orang Asli lack special privileges—unless being controlled by a government department is considered one—is obscured by their occasionally being grouped with Malays and Borneo natives as *bumiputera* ("princes of the soil," i.e., "indigenes") in official pronouncements and statistics. For example, in a Parliamentary debate on the meaning of the term *bumiputera*, then-Prime Minister Tunku Abdul Rahman pointed out that the Constitution uses it only for Borneo natives. He added that "if the term is used by the government with reference to the states of Peninsular Malaysia, it should be understood as referring exclusively to Malays and aborigines of the peninsula" (Siddique and Suryadinata 1981-1982:674). JHEOA officials also claim that Orang Asli are *bumiputera* (Jimin et al. 1983:43 n.1; Mohd Tap 1990:12). In recent Malaysia Plans—five-year plans the government uses to define development goals—the special programs for Malays and Borneo natives are said to be directed toward improving the lot of *bumiputera*, falsely implying that Orang Asli also benefit. The question of whether Orang Asli are *bumiputera* or not is a red herring which merely obscures their lack of special privileges.

Land Rights

We indigenous people aren't educated. We're not the sort of people who like pestering the government. We don't know how to beg for this subsidy here and that subsidy there from the government.

In good times and bad we look after ourselves, without bothering other people. All we want from the government is for it to do something about our petition [submitted over 30 years earlier] and gazette the land we live on.

Bah Lias k. Alang, Semai man from Perak
(Quoted in Hussein, Sivashanmugam, and
Halimaton 1991)

Last year I went to the land office to apply for land . . . "Susah. Orang Asli [Tough. You're an aborigine]," they said. "You have your own reserve. You cannot apply for Malay reserve."

But if we work and develop something—like a durian orchard—word soon gets around and [if] someone with influence applies for that land through the Land Office, he will get a title to it.

Don't look astonished. It has happened several times in my kampung [settlement]. Orang Asli have no clear rights over their land. So even if they could get the funds they have no incentive to develop it.

Long Jidin, Jakun leader (Quoted in Todd 1985)

All Orang Asli peoples have customary rights over land and resources like trees. Typically among foraging peoples like the Batek, groups claim special rights to live in particular river valleys, but willingly accept temporary incursions by other groups in times of need. Swiddening peoples like the east Semai often claim group rights to clear swiddens in an area, marked by natural landmarks, on one or both sides of a river. Fruit trees provide more individual points of attachment to the land. Mixed horticultural peoples like the Temuan consider particular groups to have more or less exclusive rights over clearly bounded tracts of land, and particular fields and trees are often owned by individuals or families. All Orang Asli have strong sentimental attachments to the land and forest in which they and their ancestors have lived. Malaysian land law incorporates customary land rights of the native Borneo peoples. However, it recognizes no Orang Asli customary land rights.

Malaysian land law rests on the British colonial "Torrens System," in which all land not individually owned by registered title deeds was "crown land," owned by the individual states in the names of the sultans. "Aboriginal lands . . . were treated as if they were unoccupied" (Means 1985-1986:640). Because Orang Asli have been, until recently, ignorant of Malaysian land laws and have not had access to government land offices, few Orang Asli have individual titles to the land they live on. Thus, almost all Orang Asli, even though living on land their ancestors occupied for many generations, are legally "squatters" on state land, as the District Officer said in the Srigala incident.

According to the Aboriginal Peoples Act, state governments can designate areas as "aboriginal areas" or "aboriginal reserves." However, this is only "enabling" legislation: they *can* create aboriginal areas and reserves, but they *do not have to*. In practice, states have been reluctant to do so. The pace of gazetting (officially announcing) Orang Asli reserves has slowed to a standstill the last two decades, except in regroupment schemes (see Chapter 5). In 1991 "only about 17 per cent of the 667 Orang Asli villages [were] gazetted as Orang Asli Areas or Reserves" (Nicholas 1991a:2; see also POASM 1991:8).[7]

Even in gazetted aboriginal reserves, Orang Asli have few rights and little security. Inhabitants of aboriginal reserves cannot obtain individual titles to land (Todd 1990:12). Therefore, Orang Asli cannot sell, lease, or mortgage the land. Nor can they use the land as collateral to obtain bank loans for making improvements on it. In most cases they cannot even get assistance from government agencies concerned with land development. They hold the land allocated to them only as "tenants at will" (Aboriginal Peoples Act, Section 8). This means that the occupant has no protection against the owner, the state, taking back the land or selling it at any time. When a state takes land from a Malay reservation, it must reserve an equal amount of land of equivalent or better quality elsewhere. No such rule applies to seizing Orang Asli land. The only improvements for which the state must pay if it takes over the land are fruit and rubber trees, and then the state decides how much to pay and which trees to pay for (Aboriginal Peoples Act, Sections 11 and 12). Orang Asli are understandably reluctant to plant trees on land that may be taken away at any time.

The JHEOA does not help Orang Asli living outside aboriginal areas and reserves obtain individual ownership of the land they live on, and it is very difficult for them to do so on their own. State land offices generally will not grant or sell land to Orang Asli, although they readily do so to Malays. The result is that Malays are often able to obtain title to land inhabited and developed by Orang Asli. In Chapter 2 we described how the Temuan of Paya Lebar lost their orchards and rice paddies to Malay neighbors. In another case, west Semai living on the Cameron Highlands Road planted rubber and fruit trees on their traditional land, with help from the JHEOA, in 1974.

> In 1979, neighbouring villagers applied for part of the Orang Asli land, and got it. When the Orang Asli protested, they were told by the Assistant District Officer to move out because the area was now "Ma-

---

7. Figures on Orang Asli land given by the JHEOA and other government agencies vary widely, leading Nicholas to describe them as "plucked from the air and tossed about" (1992a:13).

lay land" and that they were staying there illegally. After much confrontation and negotiation, extremely low compensation at $2 per rubber tree, $60 for each mature durian tree, and $20 for each petai tree was offered. However, till today, some of it is still not paid. (Nicholas 1991a:3)

We could give numerous additional examples (see, e.g., Khor 1985:281-283; Todd 1990:9; Williams-Hunt 1991; Nicholas 1991a; Dentan and Ong 1995), but the pattern is monotonously clear: Malays apply for Orang Asli land and get it; the Orang Asli are ordered to move.

Inside or outside aboriginal reserves, then, few Orang Asli have secure land tenure. This

has resulted in many Orang Asli communities losing their lands to government land schemes, private plantations, mining concessions, highway and dam projects, housing projects, recreation areas, new townships, sites for universities and various forms of "development." (Nicholas 1991a:3)

The JHEOA claims it is helpless to force states to establish Orang Asli areas and reserves (Jimin et al. 1983:67). However, Article 83 of the Constitution gives the federal government ample power to acquire land from the states, including rights over timber and minerals. It exercises this power frequently for purposes and projects it regards as important, like airports and roads. The federal government simply has not used this power to create Orang Asli areas and reserves (Rachagan 1990:103-104). This starkly illustrates the low importance the government attaches to the welfare of Orang Asli, especially since the threat of insurgency has ended. The JHEOA may be weak in its dealings with the states, but this is due in part to its lack of backing by the federal government.

Lack of Support for Orang Asli Legal Rights

The Srigala church bulldozing shows that legal and constitutional rights are meaningless if not enforced. Being a poor, undereducated, politically weak minority, Orang Asli are not in a position to demand their rights. They face powerful adversaries, including state government agencies which want to use their land or turn it over to Malays. Therefore, they must depend on their patron, the JHEOA, to put their case and uphold their interests. Unfortunately the JHEOA's support is weak.

One problem is that Orang Asli do not know their rights. The JHEOA does not take pains to inform them for fear that they will become too independent. Sometimes JHEOA officials withhold information or even lie to get Orang Asli to do what officials want. For example, JHEOA officers forced some Batek to give up lucrative jobs with logging companies on the Lebir River in the 1980s, claiming that the loggers were Communists. The real reason was that the Department does not want Orang Asli associating with Chinese (see Chapter 5).

Many Malaysians have a vested interest in keeping Orang Asli ignorant of their rights so they can more easily exploit them (Mohd Tap 1990:83-84). For example, Malay guides at the national park headquarters at Kuala Tahan in Pahang charge tourists to take them to nearby Batek villages, but they pay the Batek little or nothing in compensation for the daily disruption and humiliation of being on exhibit. Taman Negara Resort—which is partially owned by Pernas, one of many businesses owned by the ruling Malay political party, UMNO—uses a photo of a half-naked Batek boy with a blowpipe on its promotional materials and souvenirs, like T-shirts. The boy's family received about US$20 for the picture, but neither the family nor the JHEOA gave the resort permission to use it commercially.

In 1995 the boy's family asked German anthropologist Christian Vogt, who was living with the Batek and studying their world-view, to help them negotiate a royalty agreement with the resort, which he did. Outraged, the resort management and other local exploiters of the Batek reported Vogt to the police, accusing him of being a foreign agitator, "poisoning the Batek's minds," and being a "Bruno Manser in the making" (Ismail 1995; Loong 1995; Syed Azhar and Lau 1995; Vogt 1995). (Manser is the Swiss activist who embarrassed Malaysian leaders by drawing world attention to how logging was harming the Penan people of Sarawak.) This led to a major controversy, which was widely reported in the press. Vogt found himself in the absurd position of having to defend himself against charges of "instigating the Batek tribe to speak up on their rights" (*The Star* 1995a; Lau and Loong 1995). He had some local supporters, including Malays like anthropology professor Dr. Hood Salleh and the Chief Minister of Pahang, who called it "a positive sign if the Batek were concerned about their rights" (Lau and Loong 1995). Although investigations by the Pahang state government and several federal agencies determined that the charges against Vogt were baseless (*The Star* 1995a; Lau and Loong 1995), the Economic Planning Unit of the Prime Minister's Department forbade him to return to Taman Negara, thus putting a premature end to his field research. (Later the EPU stopped the resort from using the photo of the Batek boy.) One reporter questioned the justice of Vogt's research being terminated "for wanting to help the Batek" (Ismail 1995), something the JHEOA should have been doing all along.

A related problem is that the JHEOA seldom intercedes on behalf of Orang Asli even when their tormentors are breaking the law. The bulldozing of the Semai church at Teiw Srigala' was an obvious violation of their freedom of religion. But the Director-General of the JHEOA made excuses for the District Officer who ordered it done rather than taking him to court. One right that is routinely violated is Section 6(2)(iv) of the Aboriginal Peoples Act, which states that within an aboriginal area "no license for the collection of forest produce . . . shall be issued to persons not being aborigines normally resident in that aboriginal area or to any commercial undertaking without consulting the Commissioner." State governments normally grant such licenses to well-heeled, politically-connected non-Asli, who may or may not hire local Orang Asli as laborers. The JHEOA does not challenge this practice or attempt to obtain licenses on behalf of the resident Orang Asli.

One reason the JHEOA is not a strong advocate for Orang Asli rights is that most Department employees—and all those in positions of authority—are Malays (Carey 1976:299; JHEOA 1983:13; Todd 1990:12; Nicholas 1992a:10). Off the record JHEOA officials admit that the reason they cannot have Orang Asli in policy-making positions is that Orang Asli might resist the government's plans for their people (e.g., JHEOA 1983:7). In the ethnically competitive atmosphere of Malaysia, people tend to act in the interest of their own ethnic group, even when performing official duties. Thus, Orang Asli see themselves as ruled by a department of Malays acting in the interest of Malays. Semai refer sardonically to the JHEOA as *Jabatan Gop*, the "Malay Department."

Another reason the JHEOA does not strongly support Orang Asli rights is that, like any department in a government bureaucracy, its first responsibility is to carry out the orders of its political bosses. Since its beginning in the Emergency, the JHEOA's job has been to implement government plans for Orang Asli. It has never played the role of representing Orang Asli wishes to the government. All JHEOA programs are planned "top-down," by high ranking officers in the Department's Kuala Lumpur headquarters, and then implemented by state and local officials (Mohd Tap 1990:87, 92). There is no means for the people at the bottom, the Orang Asli, to initiate programs or even to give meaningful feedback. From the Department's point of view, supporting Orang Asli rights—and thereby creating a little autonomy—would only make its job of implementing government plans more difficult. Under these circumstances, the JHEOA's recurrent denunciations of Orang Asli for being "passive" and "dependent" ring hollow. To the degree this passivity and dependency actually exist, they are JHEOA creations.

THE GOVERNMENT'S GOAL FOR ORANG ASLI

The Assimilation Policy

The Ministry of the Interior's *Statement of Policy* of 1961 states that the government's goal is the "ultimate integration [of Orang Asli] with the Malay section of the community" (Ministry of the Interior 1961:3) and goes on to say that it should be "natural integration as opposed to artificial assimilation" (Ministry of the Interior 1961:5). It adds that "special measures should be adopted for the protection of the institutions, customs, mode of life, persons, property and labour of the aborigine people" (Ministry of the Interior 1961:5). It specifically advocates measures—which, however, were never implemented—to preserve and teach Aslian languages, to educate the public to counteract prejudice against Orang Asli, and to allow nomadic groups to continue their foraging life (Ministry of the Interior 1961:8, 10, 13-14). This suggests that the government envisioned Orang Asli entering into a close relationship with Malays, but remaining culturally distinct from them (Mohd Tap 1990:112-119).

In the late 1970s, however, the government began a program for converting all Orang Asli to Islam (JHEOA 1983; Mohd Tap 1990:228; see Chapter 5). This reflected a shift in the government's goal from integration to assimilation, which would result in Orang Asli being absorbed into the Malay population. Former JHEOA Director-General Jimin bin Idris stated in 1990 that he hoped the Orang Asli would become fully integrated into Malaysian society, "preferably as an Islamised subgroup of the Malays" (Todd 1990:11).

As mentioned in Chapter 1, the legal definition of a Malay is a person who speaks the Malay language, practices Malay customs, and is a Muslim. Since most Malaysians now speak Malay, and Malay customs are malleable, the definitive criterion is Islam. It is legally possible for an Orang Asli to become a Muslim and retain an Orang Asli identity (Laws of Malaysia, Act 134, Section 3 [2]), just as Muslim Indians can remain outside the Malay category. One Orang Asli group, the Orang Kuala, have been Muslims since before their arrival from Sumatra a few hundred years ago, but they adamantly maintain a separate identity from the Malays (Carey 1976:269, 276). However, government officials seem to believe that if Orang Asli can be converted to Islam, the other features will follow, and they will merge—after a few generations, anyway—into the Malay population. Indeed, the Semai phrase for converting to Islam, *moot Gop*, means "joining the Malays."

The government's current goal of turning all Orang Asli into Malays explains why it continues to administer Orang Asli under a set of laws that denies them the rights and freedoms of ordinary citizens as well as the special privileges it guarantees to other indigenous communities. The government has created a set of circumstances in which the *only way* Orang Asli can attain the rights of other indigenous citizens is by changing their ethnic identity. To Malays this may seem like a small matter. Historically Malays have readily changed their own culture as circumstances required. But Orang Asli, like most indigenous minorities around the world, are strongly opposed to giving up their religions, customs, languages, and identities. If they wanted to become Malays, they would have done so long ago. If the government's efforts are successful, "the Orang Asli will cease to exist by a process of assimilation with the Malay community. Presumably, when such assimilation is complete they will enjoy the special privileges that are accorded the Malays" (Rachagan 1990:110). Special privileges are the carrots the government holds out to entice Orang Asli to become Malays; lack of support for their rights as long as they remain Orang Asli is the stick with which the government beats them.

Reasons for the Assimilation Policy

Many Malays sincerely believe that Orang Asli would be better off as lower-class rural Malays. In theory Orang Asli converts are entitled to all the rights and privileges of Malays and should be accepted into the Malay community without prejudice. Devout Muslim Malays believe that conversion to Islam would uplift the Orang Asli, what they call "spiritual development." The Islamic revival which began in the 1970s set off a wave of proselytization, with some religious officials calling for special efforts to convert Orang Asli (see, e.g., *New Straits Times* 1988d). They apparently view Orang Asli as "softer targets" than Chinese or Indians because Orang Asli have little power to resist and because they supposedly have no religions to interfere. Government publications refer to Orang Asli religions as "superstitions" (*kepercayaan*) rather than "religions" (*ugama*). One federal official called their religions "mumbo jumbo stuff" (Datuk Chan Kong Choy, quoted in *The Star* 1993). Many Malays seem to view Orang Asli as "unfinished Malays," needing only Islam to become complete. They feel morally justified in pressuring the Orang

Asli to take a step, conversion, which they believe "is for their own good." As we have explained, the tradition of ruling class Malays imposing their ideology on Orang Asli and lower class Malays is deeply ingrained in Malay political culture (see also Dentan i.p.).

Apparently one reason the government ordered the JHEOA to begin actively promoting Islam in the late 1970s was competition between UMNO, the dominant Malay party in the ruling coalition, and PAS, the opposition Islamic Party. PAS leaders actively promoted the Iranian-inspired Islamic revival in Malaysia. To undercut the appeal of PAS to devout Muslims, UMNO mounted a campaign to infuse the public service and the Malaysian ethos with Islamic values. Its newfound zeal to bring Orang Asli into the fold was part of this larger movement (Mohd Tap 1990:228). The government was also alarmed by the success of Christian missionaries among Orang Asli, which threatened to subvert its goal of absorbing the Orang Asli into the Malay population and opened it to criticism by PAS.

An even more powerful political motive for turning all Orang Asli into Malays is that it would solve a problem for Malay leaders in their competition with Chinese and Indians. The ideological basis for the special privileges of Malays and the special economic programs to uplift *bumiputera* is that Malays, unlike Chinese and Indians, are indigenous. Many Malays, especially politicians, are unhappy about the existence of a group called the "original people," as it implies that Malays are merely another immigrant group. Indeed non-Malays often argue privately that Orang Asli, not Malays, are the true *bumiputera*, and only Orang Asli should have special privileges (Mohd Tap 1990:13). They cannot say so publicly, however, because there are laws, made possible by Article 10(4) of the Constitution, which forbid questioning the special rights of Malays. Absorbing all Orang Asli into the Malay population—making them just another subgroup of Malays—would eliminate this problem, while simultaneously augmenting the electoral strength of the Malays. As one cynical Semai put it, "when all Orang Asli have become Malays, then Malays will become Orang Asli."

Finally, assimilating indigenous minorities into the dominant ethnic group is a common nation-building tactic in developing multiethnic nations (Mohd Tap 1990:6). Thai governments have for many years tried to absorb tribal and minority groups, including the Malays of southern Thailand, into the Thai Buddhist population. This policy greatly angers Malays in Malaysia, who do not see the analogy between the Thai program and their own program for Orang Asli. In Burma, the military government has been waging war since the 1960s against tribal groups that refuse to assimilate with the Burmese. Governments like to incorporate minority groups in the national economy as low-paid workers and in the political system as subordinates. One phase of this process is to create a unifying national ideology, often based on the religion and culture of the leaders' ethnic group. "The dominant view of the ruling Malay elite is that Malay culture must form the basis for Malaysian culture" (Siddique and Suryadinata 1981-1982:684). Converting Orang Asli to Islam gives them values consonant with life as a state citizen, gives administrators a new avenue of social control, and eliminates indigenous religions that might provide a basis for resistance.

4

Development, Destruction, and Encroachment

Malaysia is as concerned as others with the global environmental degradation and the urgent need to arrest and even reverse this process of decline. Fundamental to this is the need to make the right diagnosis of the causes and problems so that the remedial measures are feasible, meaningful and implementable. Such diagnoses and remedies should be based on facts rather then emotions, reality rather than rhetoric, totality rather than piece-meal, equity rather than partiality and propriety rather than persecution.

Prime Minister Mahathir bin Mohamad (Quoted in Ministry of Primary Industries 1992:1)

Hostile nature, obstinate and fundamentally rebellious, is in fact represented in the colonies by the bush, by mosquitoes, natives, and fever, and colonization is a success when all this indocile nature has finally been tamed. Railways across the bush, the draining of swamps and a native population which is non-existent politically and economically are in fact one and the same thing.

Frantz Fanon (1968[1961]:250)

We live, always, under the power of other people. The

*government, always, uses its power not to make things
easy for us but to make them hard, one minute this way,
the next minute that, until making a living in the forest
also becomes hard. Nowadays even food is hard to come
by because now the forest isn't ours any more, it's the
government's. What we knew, in the days of our ancestors, was that the forest was ours. But now it seems that
people in the cities own the forest. And they have power
over us.*

Semai from the Regroupment Scheme at Betau in
Pahang (Quoted in Hasan Mat Nor 1989:107-108)

THE IMPACT OF ORANG ASLI ON THE ENVIRONMENT

As recently as 1962 about 75 percent of the land area of the
Peninsula was covered by primary forest of various types,
including mangrove forest, freshwater swamp forest, lowland rainforest, submontane (foothill) rainforest, and montane (mountain) forest. Lowland rainforest alone covered
about 60 percent of the Peninsula (Ooi 1963:68-84). These are
the oldest and arguably most diverse rainforests in the world.
There are almost 8000 species of flowering plants, of which
2500 are trees; 5000 species of algae, a third of the world total;
150,000 species of insects; well over 100 species of snakes;
almost 500 species of birds; over 200 species of mammals,
including 70 of bats (Hurst 1990:53). Most Orang Asli traditionally lived in forests of some kind.

If only because their numbers are small, Semang foragers
like Batek have had little impact on the forest. Swiddeners
like east Semai increased biodiversity by increasing the numbers of secondary forest species which, before agriculture,
had thrived only in areas opened up by windfalls, floods,
landslips, and other natural disasters. Gaurs, the wild cattle
of Malaysia, probably became firmly established on the Peninsula only after swiddening had made grazing lands available. Otherwise swiddening had little impact on the forest.
As long as people do not use the fields and house sites more
than a year or two, the forest restores itself in about fifteen
years, with a slight increase in the frequency of economically

valuable trees which the swiddeners have planted or spared in the course of clearing fields. A recent study by Harvard University and the Universiti Pertanian ("Agriculture University") indicates that, contrary to Forestry Department claims of widespread devastation, swiddening affected less than a tenth of one percent of Peninsular Malaysian forests (Nicholas 1992a:13).

One reason for the lack of impact is that, once swaths of secondary forest began to occur in pristine rainforest, swiddeners tended to clear them rather than primary forest, where the sheer size of the trees makes cutting them down much harder than cutting the smaller secondary forest trees. After building a platform fifteen or twenty feet above the ground to get above the buttresses, two men working together may take a full day to fell a large tree with traditional tools.

Moreover, Malaysian swiddeners have a proprietarial attitude toward the forest. Semai and Semelai, for example, try to preserve useful trees, and the number of trees to which people lay claim is enormous (Gianno 1990; Dentan and Ong 1995). Therefore, the distinction between wild and domesticated trees is less clear for Orang Asli than for their neighbors. The claim can be made that traditionally Peninsular Malaysian rainforests were Orang Asli tree farms. "Wild" fruit trees play a prominent part in traditional Orang Asli religion: heaven is full of fruit trees, for example.

This relationship is not "primitive environmentalism," but is a successful environmental adaptation, which persists because and as long as it is successful. For example, Semai in a catchment area along the Warr River (Malay Sungai Woh) were careful to preserve the surrounding forest, not merely because it would have been foolish to destroy it now that they were supposed to stay put in one place, but also because people told them that logging in a catchment area was illegal. "Then people from the Forestry Department came along and chopped down all the trees that were easy to take out. So we figured, better us than them, and we chopped down all the rest." Indeed, a few Orang Asli have allegedly made a good deal of money from logging, although only when they controlled the logging corporation. Similarly, Semelai took chain saws to their trees only when they realized that outsiders would do so if they did not (Gianno 1990:97).

The ability to coexist with the forest, in other words, is not so much a matter of "culture" as it is of money or class. The few Orang Asli who have made a lot of money from logging, like their counterparts in other ethnic groups, are not the rustic people who actually live in the forest. The latter are intelligent enough not to destroy the environment on which they depend. The attitude is practical, not cultural or "spiritual." A study of forcibly settled Semang characterizes people with this pragmatic attitude toward the forest as "primitive polluters" (Rambo 1985). The phrase is catchy. But it equates going to the grocery store with burning it to the ground, a rhetorical tactic useful only for arsonists. A recent study by the American National Academy of Sciences concluded that, wherever in the world central or state governments (rather than local people) controlled timber rights, forests were overlogged (Alper 1993:1896). The reason is that governments everywhere get the benefits from logging, in the form of concession fees and taxes, while the locals suffer the losses. As a result, the rulers seek to generate cash and jobs for the short term, while the locals take a longer range view of the forest. Malaysia is no exception.

MALAYSIAN VIEWS OF DEVELOPMENT

Religious beliefs, whether true or false, are in no way incompatible with civilization and worldly progress unless they forbid the acquisition of science, the earning of a livelihood, and progress in sound civilization. . . . If the lack of faith brought about the progress of peoples, then Arabs of the Age of Ignorance would have had to have precedence in civilization. For they were mostly followers of the materialist path. . . . They lived in utmost ignorance, like wild animals.
      Jamal al-Din al-Afghani (1973 [1880-1881]:430)

When the authorities clear the forest for rubber and oil palm schemes, it is called development; when we Orang Asli do the same thing for the growing of food crops and commercial trees, it is called forest destruction.

Anonymous Perak Semai (Quoted in *Pernloi Gah*
1991:10)

Malaysian Development Goals

The Malaysian government's basic view of development
largely corresponds to the "modernization" theories that
arose after World War II. According to Rostow's influential
"stages of economic growth" model (1960), all societies can be
placed on a continuum between undeveloped and developed. For Rostow, developing societies have to pass through
five stages: (1) traditional, (2) pre-takeoff, (3) takeoff, (4) the
drive to maturity, and (5) mass consumption. This process is
sometimes called "westernization" because the desired end
state is an industrialized society like those of the capitalist
West. Most modernization theorists believe that development requires imposing capitalist economic practices, markets, division of labor, bureaucratic rationality, modern state
structures, and "modern" technology. "Traditional" practices
and social forms must perish. Although modernization theories were much criticized in the 1970s and 1980s, they have
endured in various guises in the policies of international
agencies and national governments, including Malaysia's.

The Malaysian government's goal is to make Malaysia a
fully industrialized country with a standard of living similar
to the nations of Europe by the year 2020. Leaders picture Malaysia becoming like Singapore, but with Malays instead of
Chinese as the predominant people. They intend to increase
the population from about 18 million in 1993 to 70 million by
the year 2100. Although the ultimate goal is an economy
based on manufacturing and information industries, development planners see the expansion of primary industries,
like those the British colonial regime emphasized, as a logical
intermediate step. These include logging, mining, and plantation agriculture. The hope is that primary industries will
generate wealth to improve the infrastructure and to plow
back into manufacturing. There is not much room in such a
society for the rural lifestyle of most Orang Asli.

Especially under the leadership of Prime Minister Mahathir Mohamad, economic development has overridden all other considerations (Mitton 1995). Mahathir has been a leading advocate in international fora for the proposition that the "right to development" takes priority over such "Western" values as freedom of the press or biodiversity. Before and during the UN's 1992 "Earth Summit," Mahathir echoed American President Bush's reluctance to accept any limitations on development that might affect his own country. While Bush was defending the air pollution generated by the industrial West, Mahathir was defending his country's prodigious logging off of its tropical rainforests, both of which were criticized as destructive to the global environment.

Malay Concepts of Development

The meanings of the Malay terms used to talk about development overlap the meanings of such English terms as "growth," "development," and "progress." There are shadings of difference in the meanings of the two sets of terms, however, which may help clarify the ways in which Malays view development.

Tumbuh

One Malay term for development is *pertumbuhan*, based on the root *tumbuh*, "to grow, sprout." Its primary reference is the growth of plants. This suggests that one view of development is that it is growth due to the natural unfolding of a preordained pattern, perhaps Rostow's "stages of economic growth." Malaysian planners, like their Western counterparts, measure the progress of their development programs in terms of the growth of such economic indicators as Gross Domestic Product (GDP) and hectares of land under plantations. Some Malaysians, however—especially environmentalists and devout Muslims—object to the assumption that "bigger is always better" (see, e.g., Samir Amin 1991).

Bangun

Another Malay term for development is *pembangunan*, from the root *bangun*, "to get up, rise to an upright position, build." The connotation is that development is the construction of an upright structure. In this conception, the Malay rulers see themselves as the architects who must direct and motivate the workers, the mass of traditionally minded commoners, to build the new structure. It also implies that the enlightened ruling class must "arouse" or "awaken" (*membangunkan*) the people themselves in order to achieve development. This is similar to the ideas of modernization theorists who emphasize the need for changing the mentality of the people who are to be developed, for example, to make them more "achievement" oriented (McClelland 1962).

The special Malay emphasis is on the notion that development is something that rulers do to and for their subjects. The top-down, patron-client connotation implicit in the term *membangunkan* pervades Malaysian discussion of development. Development is something a superior person does for an inferior, as an expression of superiority. The proper response is gratitude, because, in Malay feudalism, superiors bestow care on their inferiors as a gift, not an obligation. Largesse is always, in a sense, a surprise, not an expectation.

Semai contrast their own custom of accepting favors without comment—because one expects friends to do each other favors—with the Malay custom of thanking a benefactor by saying *terima kasih*, "receive affection." The salience of the patron-client conception of development in the minds of the ruling class shows up in the drumbeat of complaints in speeches by officials berating peasants, especially Malay peasants, for ingratitude and urging them not to depend on the government. As we show in Chapter 5, Department of Aboriginal Affairs officers have the same attitude toward Orang Asli whom they are trying to "develop."

Maju and Moden

Another Malay term for development is *kemajuan*, whose root, *maju*, means "to advance, move forward, improve, progress." These terms equate development with English

concepts like "advancement" and "progress." A closely related term is *moden*, from English "modern," which has similarly positive connotations. Development, then, is pictured as
progressive and modern, by contrast with traditional practices. Officials often denounce such practices as swiddening
simply because they are not "advanced," not because they are
ineffective.

A major difference between Malay and Western concepts
of progress is that the Malay idea has a religious dimension.
The idea of "progress" became salient in European thinking
during the Enlightenment. At that time, it was one of the
ideological weapons with which intellectuals beat the Church
(Bury 1932:144-172). They saw Christianity as impeding secular progress. In Malaysia, ruling class Malays regard Islam
as an important aspect of being "progressive." In the development of Pasisir Malay culture, "advanced" (*maju*) civilization came through west coast trading ports. After the
thirteenth century, these coastal enclaves became Muslim.
Most "progressive" ideas and practices passed through an Islamic filter before entering Malay culture. Social problems
Westerners traditionally regard as "the price of progress"
seem to most Malays to be results of uncritical borrowing
from the decadent (secular) West, rather than entailments of
capitalist economic development. Real *kemajuan* should have
an Islamic coloration.

Orang Asli, Malaysian developers and JHEOA officials
agree, are *kurang maju*, "rather backward." They see economic modernization programs and Islamization as equally necessary for "developing" the Orang Asli (see Chapter 5).

Environmental Protection

> *Which is more important—the development of a condo-
> minium or the safety of the people and environment?*
> Deputy Prime Minister Datuk Seri Anwar Ibra-
> him (Quoted in *Utusan Konsumer* 1994b:10)

> *We could not spare the time for the EIA [Environmental
> Impact Assessment] then. In the rush to develop the
> island, certain allowances had to be made. There was no*

favouritism.

Tan Sri Haji Osman Aroff, Chief Minister of
Kedah (Quoted in *The Star*, June 11, 1992)

Malaysia has enacted some regulations intended to protect
the environment from the side-effects of development. But,
because development is a higher priority than the environment to government leaders, the laws are seldom enforced.

The Environmental Quality Act (Amended) of 1985 requires sponsors of nineteen types of development projects,
including the most destructive ones, to assess the impact of
the project on the environment. Forestry, housing, mining,
and building infrastructure are included. The initiator of the
project does the EIA, since the Department of the Environment lacks the money, expertise, and staff to conduct its own
assessment. The Department can publish an EIA and invite
public comment, but usually does not. The Prime Minister
continues to support the law in his public speeches (*Utusan
Konsumer* 1992b:20).

As in the United States over the last decade or so, lax or
corrupt enforcement has undermined the intent of the law.
The initiator tends to see the impact of the development in a
rosy light. For example, the EIA for a golf resort on Redang
Island off the east coast of the Peninsula envisioned tripling
sedimentation at a local delta and providing 1500 local jobs;
the sedimentation was sextupled and only a hundred or so
jobs resulted. Satellite imaging also revealed illegal clearing
of mangrove forest (*Utusan Konsumer* 1992a:9). A pipeline to
deliver 300,000 gallons of water to the resort daily (200,000 of
that for watering the golf course, the rest for five-star hotels)
involved no EIA at all (*Utusan Konsumer* 1993a:4). The Deputy
Minister of Science, Technology, and the Environment, ad-
mitting the illegal logging for the first time, claimed that the
developer had replanted the mangrove, a claim that *Utusan
Konsumer* carried in its "Ha! Ha!" column in mid-November
of 1992.

There are other Malaysian environmental laws whose enforcement would benefit not only Orang Asli but other Malaysians as well. State authorities' non-enforcement of the
Land Conservation Act 1960 and the National Forestry Act
1984 has facilitated indiscriminate clearing of hill land. Al-

though the former makes no provision for degazetting hill land, states have been doing so to allow development (*Utusan Konsumer* 1994a:6). The people who suffer most are those who traditionally have lived on steep forested hills—the Orang Asli.

MALAYSIAN DEVELOPMENT IN PRACTICE

Logging the Rainforest

> *The development boom in the past two decades when land was extensively cleared for housing, infrastructure and industry has contributed to flood woes in Kuala Lumpur.*
> T. M. Jayarajan, Director, Kuala Lumpur Drainage and Sewerage Department (Quoted in *Malay Mail*, October 22, 1991)

> *The needs of the Orang Asli should especially be taken into consideration in the case of forestry exploitation.*
> Then Deputy Prime Minister Datuk Musa Hitam (Quoted in *The Star*, November 28, 1982)

> *Our fruit trees were destroyed, our ancestor's graves were desecrated, and our water supply polluted. No compensation at all was paid. The timber company [Syarikat Bensen Timber and Trading of Bentong] also promised to pay us $5,000 for the construction of an access road but this has still to be fulfilled.*
> Bah Ramli knoon Bah Ngum, a Pahang Semai (Quoted in Nicholas 1991b:4)

The Economics and Politics of Logging

The development activity with the harshest impact on Orang Asli is logging, a prerequisite to most development projects. Although Malaysia is well known for its export of manufactures, palm oil, rubber, and tin, the two exports which made it the most money in the 1980s were oil and timber. Malaysia's reputation for reckless destruction of rainforest stems largely from its activities in Sabah and Sarawak, which are beyond the scope of this report. There is, however, nothing about agroforestry in Peninsular Malaysia that would modify the country's notoriety. Loggers removed roughly 300,000 hectares of forest per year during the 1970s and 200,000 per year in the early 1980s before the government, fearing total depletion of timber supplies, restricted cutting to 149,000 hectares per year (Hurst 1990:50). (One hectare is 2.471 acres.) In 1978 loggers were clearing almost two acres per minute (Singh 1981:181).

Malaysians point out that they practice selective logging in contrast with the clearcutting American companies do. Nor does the Malaysian government provide the infrastructure for logging in government forest reserves the way the U.S. government does. Still, selective logging of less than a third of the trees in Malaysian rainforest destroys half to three quarters of the canopy, in large part due to the roads needed to get the timber down the steep slopes. Supposedly the relevant state forestry department will check whether replacement or enrichment planting is necessary, but in fact such inspection rarely occurs (Hurst 1990:68).

Control over logging lies with state governments, which have many incentives to maximize it. Not only do state governments receive indirect profits from logging and other development in the form of taxes and concessionary fees, but also many members of the ruling class profit directly. The states do not auction off timber concessions, but let them go to people with the proper political connections. The state of Pahang, home to more Orang Asli than any other state, is an egregious example of how Malaysian agroforestry works in practice. The state government routinely gives logging concessions and authorizes logging for development without even the fig leaf of an Environmental Impact Assessment. Many of these projects go to foreign investors with even less interest in environmental quality than the state government. Illegal logging is so rampant in the state that the state forestry department announced that it was out of control. But the Auditor-General revealed in December, 1992, that the "chief culprits" in logging outside their concessions were companies the state government had set up. The Chief Minister said that he was unaware of the illegal actions. Meanwhile, the Sultan of Pahang and his enormous family put "tremendous pressure on the government to give them more timber land than the 37,223.6 ha of concessions the Sultan received between 1988 and July, 1992" (*Utusan Konsumer* 1992c:6). The Sultan and his family have vast timber allotments, and they have expanded them into forest reserves and game reserves without any protest from the supine state Forestry Department.

The only category of forest truly immune to the threat of logging is national parks. The only national park in Peninsular Malaysia is the 4340 square kilometer Taman Negara, which the British established as a wildlife sanctuary in 1939. Overlapping the borders between Pahang, Kelantan, and Trengganu, it falls within the traditional territory of the Batek, for whom it has become a refuge from logging outside the park.

A good example of logging for development in Pahang is the 2000 hectare (5000 acre) Taiwanese eel farm development in a peat swamp forest near Nenasi (*Utusan Konsumer* 1992d, 1992e). Malaysian peat forest is a distinctive community, and hardly any virgin peat forest is left (Ibrahim and Chong 1992). The Pahang State Development Corporation approved the project in January, 1988, six months before Malaysian law required Environmental Impact Assessments for large projects of this kind. The state leased the land to the developers as a shrimp farm, which would use sea water, but around 1990 the developers decided to make it the largest eel farm in the world and constructed about 400 deep water wells to pump freshwater twenty-four hours a day. The fact that shrimp farming in Taiwan itself is a disaster may have inspired the change. The effects of the eel farm on the hydrology of the area are unknown. The Chief Minister of Pahang says that critics of the project are "jealous" of the state's ability to attract foreign investment.

Orang Asli have no influence on logging decisions even when they concern Orang Asli reserves. The experience of Bah Ramli's people (see epigraph above), whose lands were given away by the Pahang Forestry Department without the people's knowledge, let alone their consent, is typical. Even the minuscule amounts of compensation loggers promise Orang Asli often go unpaid.

In another typical case, a Temuan community in Negri Sembilan "applied to log their own 200-acre reserve and the adjacent 340 acres of forest. . . . They planned to use the profits to plant more rubber and durian orchards, and rebuild their dilapidated houses" (Todd 1990:11). But the license was given to a Malay businessman, who engaged a Chinese company to do the logging. Despite the Temuan headman's protests to the JHEOA, the state forestry department, and the Chief Minister of the state, the outside company carried out the logging. The Temuan received nothing except pollution in their water supply. The businessman even cheated the Temuan out of the meager compensation they were owed for the loss of their fruit trees by forging the illiterate headman's signature on a letter saying his community had received M$42,000 (Todd 1990:11).

Finally, in any place where one or two trees can be worth a poor family's annual income, there will be a lot of illegal logging. Even in Europe and America black walnut trees are traditional targets for thieves (Little 1980:359). The world demand for tropical timber, which drives governments and legal entrepreneurs, also drives thieves. Illegal logging is rampant in the state of Kelantan, especially in the Gua Musang and Jeli areas, where Temiar, Mendriq, and Jahai live. Timber thieves have no time for Orang Asli sensibilities. They bulldoze roads through graveyards and orchards, pollute the rivers, and clear-cut the forest. They sleep with Temiar women and let the people watch pornographic movies and Hulk Hogan on video with them. They often have papers purporting to allow them to clear the forest (Saiful 1991). Also in Kelantan, a renegade logging company bulldozed a road into the upper Aring River (in Batek country), deep inside Taman Negara, and took out all the accessible choice trees, leaving devastation behind.

Semai watch the illegal loggers, who are mostly Chinese, with wry amusement: "There used to be a lot of Koompassia trees around here, but the Chinese stole them, every last one [*laughs*]." State forestry departments claim that they lack the resources to patrol the forest. And there is enough loose money connected with logging that corruption in the departments is commonplace.

The Aftermath of Logging

The effects of logging in tropical forest are well known. The absence of shade raises the temperature of the soil to desert conditions, so that it no longer holds water well and easily blows away. In the dry season, the result downstream may be a drought, reducing the amount of water available for irrigation. Since there are no roots to hold the thin, dusty topsoil in place, heavy rains then flush the topsoil into the rivers. Mud bars choke the rivers, making them unavailable for transportation and killing the more sensitive fish on which rural people depend for food. Siltation reduces the life of hydroelectric projects. During the monsoons, the rivers' reduced carrying capacity leads to flooding. As early as 1977, human activity accounted for about a fifth of the 2 million cubic liters of silt carried by the Kelantan River, which originates in Temiar and Semang territory. Studies in Kelantan indicate that logging a third of a catchment area triples sedimentation in the rivers; selective felling throughout the area increases sedimentation twenty-five-fold (Hurst 1990:51).

Logging roads, even more than loss of trees, cause erosion. Exposed to torrential rains, the soft laterite soil washes away as soon as the loggers move on. Logging roads also interrupt natural drainage, creating stagnant pools, ideal breeding places for the mosquitoes that carry malaria. Often the land is left too eroded to allow the forest to regenerate. Eventually, the succession is to grassland, typically of useless *lalang* grass.

Malaysia's plan for "replanting the forest" involves three species of trees, not 5000; there is no way to restore the forests' diversity (Hurst 1990:64; Dentan and Ong 1995:60). Except for a few tiny patches, lowland rainforest and peat swamp forest are extinct in Peninsular Malaysia. Mangrove forest is going rapidly. Submontane and montane forest should be in the same condition as the lowland rainforest before the end of the century.

Its insistence to the contrary notwithstanding, the Malaysian government is sensitive to outside criticism of its logging policies. Most of its response is in the area of public relations rather than of forestry. At the "Indigenous People's Conference" in late 1993, for example, the Ministry of Primary Industries distributed a large, glossy booklet, featuring lots of green ink and beautiful pictures, titled *Forever Green: Malaysia and Sustainable Forest Management* (Ministry of Primary Industries 1992). On p. 18 begins the typical denunciation of "radical NGOs and environmentalists" as outside agitators who instigate indigenous peoples "to go against the law of their nation," e.g., by blockading logging roads. The obligatory denunciation of swidden horticulture is on p. 20. The government-controlled press routinely runs stories lauding the government's "green" policies and denouncing meddling foreign environmentalists, represented as dupes or conscious agents of Western timber interests or as radicals who want to keep forest-dwelling indigenous people as "museum specimens" for Western tourists to goggle at. Malaysians who protest government policies abroad are "traitors." Those at home may be subject to indefinite detention without trial under the Internal Security Act (Hurst 1990:71).

Logging destroys not only the natural resources of the forest which Orang Asli depend upon, but also some of their most important "capital investments," their fruit trees. Loggers treat trees which indigenous people have planted or tended in the forest as "wild" and therefore ignore the laws requiring that they pay fair compensation for destroying people's productive trees. The loggers who cleared the area around Mncak, a Semai settlement near Kampar, never paid the headman the fee promised: "Not dime one," he says with a wry smile. Though the logging took place years ago, erosion caused by logging roads continues to damage crops. Complaints to the JHEOA bring no response.

Indeed, it may take confrontation of the sort from which Orang Asli usually shrink to bring about a settlement in which they get compensation even for the timber value of the trees—the equivalent of paying the owner of a destroyed factory the value of the raw materials from which the factory was constructed. For example, in 1982, in northeast Pahang, Semai near Bukit Seruk held 1000 tons of logs hostage to protest logging on their reserve by a company from Johore. The logging was legal, since the state had issued a concession to the company, despite having refused one to the Semai who had applied a couple of years before. An earlier logging project, completed in 1980, was supposed to pay them M$55,000 (the value of a couple of dozen high-priced hardwood trees), but they received only M$32,000. This time they wanted a good road, water, and electricity (Farush Khan 1982a, 1982b). Without publicity, the state government agreed to the demands. Eventually, they got a road. The water supply went only to the school, however, and there was still no electricity by 1985, although every house in a nearby FELDA project (a Malay settlement) had its own electricity and water supply (Todd 1985).

There is no indication that, without such confrontations, any developer, public or private, will follow the former Deputy Prime Minister's exhortation, quoted at the beginning of this section, to take the needs of Orang Asli into account.

Laying the Blame for Deforestation

> *Just because most of them are illiterate, uneducated and have no political connections, one should not take advantage of the Orang Asli and pin the blame on them for things which they did not do.*
> JHEOA Director-General speaking to Orang Asli in Perak (Quoted in *Pernloi Gah* 1991a:10)

Incredibly, forestry departments and state governments often blame Orang Asli for deforestation (Ministry of Primary Industries 1992:20-21). Swiddening—"slash and burn agriculture"—is the main scapegoat, although swiddening went on for centuries "without producing anything like the destruction that a few years of 'controlled, selective' logging under Forestry Department supervision produced" (Dentan and Ong 1995:77-78). Swiddening has actually been declining during precisely the time that deforestation has risen. Along the R'eis River (Malay Sungai Rias) in 1991-1992, for example, only one of several Semai settlements had any swiddens, and even there only a few families participated. One settlement no longer even had a shaman qualified to perform the swidden-opening rituals.

Officials also accuse Orang Asli of "encroaching" on the forest. For example, a Semai headman in Perak wrote five letters to state authorities (including the Forestry Department) over the course of two years announcing that, as urged by the government, his people were going to clear twenty acres of forest on their traditional lands, so they could plant tree crops and build a permanent settlement, in effect abandoning swiddening. Receiving no reply, they had gone ahead with the plan. The Perak state government, backed by the Perak-Kedah branch of the JHEOA, accused the group of "encroaching" on state land and destroying state forest. The headman was shocked at his group being labeled "encroachers" on land their ancestors had occupied for generations. The chairman of the Perak branch of the Orang Asli Association (POASM) complained that, while outsiders continued to log illegally in Orang Asli areas, it was only the Orang Asli who were called "encroachers" (Nicholas 1991b:2).

The figures the Perak Forestry Department uses to indict the Orang Asli are apparently made up out of whole cloth. It claimed in July, 1989, that "to date," Orang Asli had destroyed 25,000 hectares of forest, costing the state M$22.2 million; in April, 1991, the amount the Orang Asli had supposedly destroyed was less, 22,000 hectares, but the value far more, M$93.4 million. In Perak, legal logging covers 12,000 hectares annually, so generations of Orang Asli "encroachment" amounted to about two years of legal log production (Nicholas 1992c). There may be a clue to these discrepancies in the nickname by which, without conscious irony, Perak Semai refer to the state Forestry Department: *maay glgiil jhuu'*, "the people who chop down trees."

Tree Plantations and FELDA Schemes

Tree Plantations

Many development projects involve arboriculture (tree crops): primarily rubber and oil palm, but also cocoa, coffee, and fruit trees. Funding for tree plantations comes either from the private sector, often with formal or informal government participation, or from government rural development agencies like FELDA (Federal Land Development Authority).

The ruling class represents plantations as environmentally responsible. Signs line the road into Kuala Lumpur from the airport: "WE GREEN THE EARTH";[1] smaller print identifies the trees by the side of the road as rubber or oil palm. Plantations of fast growing softwoods for logging covered only 6750 hectares by 1984. The government proposes to vastly increase this area (Hurst 1990:50). The Forestry Department counts these plantations as forest, by the same logic that would classify Iowa cornfields as grassland.

Still, even monocrop plantation trees do recycle CO_2, screen the soil from direct sunlight and torrential monsoon rains, and retain a fairly constant temperature and humidity at ground level. They perform none of these functions as well as a mature rainforest, however; cannot sustain themselves; and of course drastically reduce biodiversity. Soil loss is only double that of rainforest, as opposed to a twenty-fold increase for tea plantations and a thirty-fold increase for vegetable production (Hurst 1990:51). In terms of preserving the environment, logging to produce single-species tree plantations is a step up from logging for other purposes.

FELDA Schemes

The Federal Land Development Authority (FELDA) oversees agricultural development schemes for poor or landless peasants. Almost all beneficiaries are Malays. The British established the agency in 1956 during the Emergency to undercut the appeal of Communism to peasants displaced by British development schemes, especially rubber plantations. The program was always political. In colonial days preference was given to members of the Malay "Home Guard," a pro-British paramilitary organization. Observers agree that political connections are still useful in getting admitted to a FELDA scheme (Hurst 1990:65-67). Orang Asli usually lack such connections.

Early FELDA schemes provided each resettled family with a plank house and 4.5 hectares of land planted in oil

---

1.   The Indonesian government similarly took out advertisements proclaiming its devotion to "greenness" on CNN in November, 1993.

palm or rubber. Families owned their own crops, but participated in joint harvesting. FELDA built the infrastructure:
schools, roads, clinics. Recent FELDA schemes are coopera-
tives in which the coop owns the land—except for the house
plots—and the members work for wages, essentially as rural
proletarians.

Between 1970 and 1985 FELDA cleared about 100,000
hectares of forest annually. From 1985 to 1990 it planned on
clearing 60,000 hectares a year (Hurst 1990:50). This is not selective logging. After the valuable trees have been removed,
the rest of the vegetation is cut and burned off. Bulldozers re-
contour the bare earth before rubber trees or oil palms are
planted.

The main effect of private plantations and FELDA
schemes on Orang Asli is to displace them from their land.
For example, the government cleared 5000 acres of Orang
Asli traditional land for an oil palm plantation in Kampung
Cawang in Perak, leaving 100 acres of forest. FELDA schemes
often bring displacement without compensation, as happened to Semai near Sahom in Perak.

Luring Golfers, Tourists, and the Select Few

*A lifestyle, so leisurely and so gracious that, thankfully,
it can be enjoyed by only a select few.*
Advertisement for the Sultan Aziz Shah Golf
Club

*As a tour manager who has made repeated visits to
Malaysia over the past eight years, I would like to comment on what I feel is the deteriorating condition of one of
your premier tour destinations.*

*Far from being a "beauty spot" being cared for and nur-
tured in the hope of sustaining long-term development,
Cameron Highlands is being ravaged by developers in
search of quick profits from building high-rise flats and
apartments.*

*Please, Malaysia, don't make the mistake of ignoring
beauty in the rush to expand your tourism industry.*
"Steve" (from London) (Letter to the *New Straits
Times*, August 16, 1993. Also quoted in *Utusan
Konsumer* 1994b:11)

Golf courses are particularly hard on the natural environment, but most of the damage they do is of the same sort that other kinds of development do. The Malaysian government is giving grants of M$200,000 to districts (*daerah*) to build more of them. It is therefore worth looking at them as exemplars of devastating development.

Tourism is big business in Malaysia. Resorts and golf courses, which go together in Malaysia like rice and curry, constitute a major industry (*Utusan Konsumer* 1991:6; APPEN 1990). Throughout the 1980s, the Deputy Prime Minister repeatedly praised golf as a game and golf courses as a form of development (NNP 1992, 1993b). By 1990 there were about 75 golf courses in Malaysia, with plans for 200 by the year 2000.

The benefits of golf courses flow mostly to state governments, developers, and wealthy locals and foreigners. In 1990 yearly membership fees ranged from US$10,000 to US$30,000. That year the mean annual per capita income in Malaysia was about US$2250 (*Utusan Konsumer* 1993b, 1993c). In Japan, however, membership fees ran over US$100,000 a year. In land-poor Singapore and Hong Kong, fees were also high. It was cheaper for a group of rich Japanese or overseas Chinese to charter an airplane, fly to Malaysia, rent rooms in a luxurious resort and play golf there than to stay at home and play. A quarter of the members of the Templer Park Country Golf Club and 30 percent of the Rahman Golf Club were Japanese (NNP 1993a).

It is ordinary Malaysians, however, who bear the costs of golf courses. Besides displacing indigenous peoples, usually without significant compensation, golf courses devastate the environment. Not counting the ancillary hotels, casinos, and so on, a golf course may require clearing 100 to 600 acres of land (*Utusan Konsumer* 1993b). Clear cutting on Malaysia's steep mountain slopes leads to erosion, with siltation and pollution of headwaters of rivers. Bulldozing the steep slopes into gradients suitable for golf requires dumping tons of raw material down slope. Exterminating indigenous weeds and preventing natural succession vegetation from taking hold requires enormous lacings with herbicides. A golf course uses a couple of tons of pesticides a year, eight or nine times the amount used on an irrigated rice field of the same size (*Utusan Konsumer* 1992f). Keeping the imported grass healthy on soils now depleted of most nutrients requires lavish applications of chemical fertilizers, of which about 90 percent end up in the air (Pratap Chatterjee 1993). To coagulate the soil underneath the water hazards builders use acrylamid, which can cause disorders of the central nervous system when it leaks into ground water (Pratap Chatterjee 1993).

The heavy rains flush this compost of bulldozer tailings, weed poison, and chemicals down the steep slopes into rivers which already carry huge amounts of silt. Chemicals poison the fish or make them unfit to eat. Country people, who use the rivers for transportation and drinking water and the fish for food, suffer. There is no forest to moderate the impact of the rain or to absorb any of the runoff, so flooding is becoming an ever more serious problem.

In dry season, the imported grass requires constant watering, about 200,000 gallons a day on the average golf course (*Utusan Konsumer* 1993a). The tropical sun evaporates a good deal of that water and the rainwater which the forest would otherwise conserve. As a result, the mud-clogged rivers now are more likely than before to run dry in dry season.

By mid 1993 the federal Environment Ministry had begun to express worry about the erosion, land clearing, soil contamination, and water pollution associated with the proliferation of golf courses in Malaysia. But state governments continued to promote them (*New Straits Times*, July 6, 1993).

Golf resorts affect Orang Asli more than they affect other Malaysians, not just because taking land on which Orang Asli live is relatively easy, but also because Orang Asli are more likely to live in the hills. Since foreign golfers tend to come from countries cooler than Malaysia, they prefer to golf at higher, cooler altitudes. As a result, the temptation is always to site a course in the highlands, despite the difficult terrain and the resulting environmental problems. In the Cameron Highlands, the heartland of Semai country, developers have cleared so much forest for golf courses that the ambient temperatures have risen a couple of degrees, imperiling the local vegetable industry, which employs a good deal of Semai occasional labor (*Utusan Konsumer* 1994b).

For Orang Asli, the benefits of developing golf courses and resorts are indirect at best. It takes two or three hundred workers to build a golf course, but only about forty to run it, fewer if it is mechanized. A few Semai with the equivalent of a high school diploma have jobs at resorts in the Cameron Highlands. In general, however, these jobs are no better than the ones they replace: occasional labor as rural proletarians collecting forest products or working in the fields. The fifty-odd Btsisi' who moved from Carey Island to the Klang waterfront in search of a better life are happy that they were not relocated to make room for the golf resort, esplanade, and factories in the North Klang Straits industrial zone next to their settlement. The resort plans to add floating chalets, apartments, bungalows, and a seafood restaurant costing about M$56 million in the next few years. So far there have been no jobs for Btsisi'. The only infrastructural benefit is that they can now get drinking water from a fire hydrant located some distance from their settlement. The amenities supplied the golfers—running water, electricity, and so on—do not extend next door to the Btsisi' (Selva 1991).

Dams

The government builds dams for flood control and for generating electricity. The lakes which dams form offer recreational opportunities for city people. Developers of resorts often build golf courses in the catchment areas around the lakes, thus compounding the destruction of the natural environment.

The best place to site a dam is in a narrow valley of the sort which, in Malaysia, is commonest in the highlands where many Orang Asli live. As a result, dams hurt Orang Asli disproportionately more than other Malaysians. Orang Asli rarely benefit from these projects. The Linggui Dam in Johore, which provides water and electricity to Singapore, flooded 5000 hectares of traditionally Jakun land. Another

14,600 hectares became catchment areas on which Jakun are not supposed to farm or build. The government agreed to pipe water into Jakun settlements from the lake which had submerged their traditional sources of water as well as their means of livelihood (Nicholas 1991c). There was no arrangement for providing electricity to Jakun. The Department of Aboriginal Affairs resettled Orang Asli displaced by the Temenggor Dam in the remote Banun area of Perak. As in most regroupment schemes (see Chapter 5), they got a school, clinic, and some plank houses. They were promised rubber trees, but did not receive them. Many men left the area looking for occasional wage labor. With no source of cash to buy food, those who stayed opened swiddens, prompting the usual chorus of complaints about how Orang Asli reject progress and practice destructive outmoded agriculture (Todd 1985).

Roads and Other Improvements

Roads

All these forms of development require roads, as do the airports and other infrastructural improvements associated with development. Logging roads do more damage to the forest than the logging itself: on the average, clearing a square mile of forest takes thirteen square miles of logging roads, not counting the skid tracks down which loggers drag the trees to the roads (Hurst 1990:68). The bulldozing does the same ecological damage that bulldozing golf courses does. The ruling class denies targeting any particular community for expropriation in building roads, but since many roads serve loggers and golf resorts, many pass through Orang Asli traditional territories, including Orang Asli reserves.

For example, the unfinished road through Temiar country from Gua Musang in Kelantan to the Lojing Highlands and on through Semai country to the North-South Highway, with a branch to the Cameron Highlands, has already created serious and extensive environmental destruction. It will facilitate the construction of more resorts in the Cameron Highlands and new ones in the Lojing Highlands and along the Temiar-Semai border. About 46,000 hectares of hill forest are to be turned into resorts and agricultural projects (*New Straits Times* 1988b, 1988c).

Tourist roads like this offer little to Orang Asli, but Orang Asli do ask the government for roads to connect their settlements with markets for their products. Such roads also facilitate administration and surveillance by government agencies. But even roads built to promote Orang Asli development benefit non-Asli traders and middlemen more than Orang Asli. They do facilitate the out-migration of young men who get rural proletarian jobs elsewhere, but wages are usually too low to permit them to remit money to their kinsmen at home. The result is often an increase in dependency on the government (Hood Salleh and Hasan Mat Nor 1984).

The impact of road-building on Orang Asli is illustrated in the case of the Orang Asli Reserve near Sahom in Perak (Dentan 1993). The British built the first north-south highway through it many years ago, following an old ox cart path. That opened up the area for tin dredging, and a large pit mine swallowed up part of the reserve. After Independence the government ran a hydroelectric powerline through the reserve, cutting an enormous swath through Orang Asli orchards. Part of the area just south of the reserve, traditionally Semai territory, went for a scheme to resettle poor peasants, although no peasants occupied the land as of 1992. Finally, a new superhighway ran straight through the reserve, leaving just a fringe of orchard on either side.

Clearly, the local Semai lost a lot of land in these projects. It seems fair to ask what benefits they gained. Bus service from the main market town does not extend past the last Malay settlement in the valley, at Sahom, but Semai can walk down the old road into Sahom to catch the bus. The school bus also goes no farther than Sahom, so schoolchildren must walk a mile or more, rain or shine, to catch the bus. Attendance at school is sporadic. Electrification also stops at Sahom. Semai are not surprised: not even the mail gets past Sahom, despite repeated requests, which the local post office does not bother to answer.

Since the government claims to own the reserve, it paid no compensation for the lost land. It did let Semai build houses on the fill made from rock blasted out of the mountains as the highway went through. The new land is sterile, but it is better than nothing. Moreover, the government paid for the destruction of those species of trees which Malays also commercially cultivate. Such trees are the component of Semai agroforestry whose existence the government acknowledges. Officials took into account the age and size of the tree, etc., in determining the amount of the owner's loss. The valuation seems also to have taken into account the ethnicity of the planters, unless one assumes that Malay trees are consistently more productive than Semai trees under the same arboricultural regime, a contention Semai vigorously contest. At any rate, documents in Dentan's possession indicate that Malays got more money for the same sort of trees.

The Sepang Airport

The 800 Temuan on or near an Orang Asli reserve in Sepang and Labu in Selangor are relatively well off compared with other Orang Asli. Government officials regularly take visiting VIPs to the area to show them a "typical" Orang Asli settlement. They have a paved road, electricity, water, a primary school, and mature orchards.

The government plans to relocate them and destroy their settlements in order to make way for a 10,000 hectare international airport (Nicholas 1991d; Tan 1993). "The new airport is bad for poor people because their land is used," said Temuan Utok Deris. "In the last 10 years, a lot of things have been done. We have only recently begun to harvest what we have planted. It is not fair to ask us to move now" (quoted in Nicholas 1991d:6). The Chief Minister of Selangor, however, referred to them as "squatting" on land needed for the first runway, although Temuan have lived there since 1810, and 891 acres is a gazetted Orang Asli reserve. The reserve land is worth US$10,000 to US$24,000 an acre, which need not be paid since Orang Asli reserves belong to the government (*The Star* 1992b; Nicholas 1992d).

Lacking legal land owning status, the Temuan turned for help to the United Malays National Organization (UMNO), the most powerful political party in the country, the party

which repeatedly claims to speak for Orang Asli and which
routinely takes almost all their votes:

> We helped UMNO establish itself here. . . . The
> UMNO branch asked for our help on many occa-
> sions. We worked hard to build a model kampung.
> We contributed to their cultural programme, even
> joined the choir and sang UMNO songs. But now . . .
>
> (A Temuan man, quoted in Nicholas 1991d:6)

UMNO offered no assistance.

The Temuan should not have been surprised. Bukit Lanjan, the other Temuan settlement which the government uses
to display how Orang Asli live, is now to be submerged in a
massive housing estate. When Europeans first arrived in Malaysia, the people were living in what is now Melaka Street in
Kuala Lumpur, the capital. Since then they have been repeatedly moved for the convenience of others: first to what is now
the Selangor Club, then to Bukit Nenas, then to Sungai Pen-
cala, and finally, around the turn of the century, to Bukit Lanjan (Williams-Hunt 1991:12).

This sort of saga is common for Orang Asli. If Orang Asli
are "nomads," as some developers argue, development is one
of the reasons.

Effects of Development on Orang Asli[2]

Displacement and Loss of Land

> *Orang Asli in Perak seem to be treated like new immi-*
> *grants to this country. To say we are encroachers in our*
> *own land is to say that we have less rights to be here than*
> *the illegal immigrants.*
>
> Alang Sabak, Chairman of the Perak Orang Asli
> Association (Quoted in Nicholas 1991b:2)

2. For further information on the effects of development on Orang
    Asli, see Endicott 1979b, 1982; Gomes 1982, 1990, 1991; Hood Salleh
    1984, 1990; Dentan 1992; Aiken and Leigh 1992:98-101; Nicholas
    1994; Dentan and Ong 1995.

One of the major effects of development of all kinds has been to displace Orang Asli from their land. Most of the hill land taken for development was until the last few decades used only by Orang Asli. Since they have no legal land tenure and since they are few, planners rarely consider them or their needs, except sometimes as nuisances to be moved out of the way. They get one reference in the Second Outline Perspective Plan (1991-2000) and one in the Sixth Malaysia Plan (1991-1995), simply acknowledging that, somehow, they have not benefited as much as other Malaysians from development. "Despite this recognition, however, there appears to be no specific plan to reverse the situation for Orang Asli. There are no assurances, for example, that Orang Asli lands—a key determinant in Orang Asli progress—will be legally recognised as being theirs to develop and use" (Nicholas 1991b:1).

We have already discussed the legal situation which allows the government to seize Orang Asli land without compensation and transfer it to developers. Because Orang Asli are few and because they rarely protest, politicians often ignore their complaints. The JHEOA is a small and rather despised player in the politics of land development, having little power to protect Orang Asli interests (Gomes 1990:24-25).

For example, in 1990 the Pahang state government seized sixty acres of land in a Temuan village for a Malay settlement and a Boy Scout training ground. When the Temuan residents complained to their state assemblyman, he first replied that he did not know that there were any Orang Asli there and promised to cancel the project. In March 1991 he told the JHEOA Director-General and the Deputy Prime Minister in charge of the Department that he would see to it that no individual or agency took the land. But the development of the Temuan land continued. Meanwhile the local JHEOA office in Bentong informed the Temuan that they had no right to the land on which their settlement stood (Nicholas 1991b:3).

In Bidor in Perak a Semai community lost most of its land and fruit trees to a tin mining company and a government agricultural project. The JHEOA then told them they would have to move because there was too little land for them.

"Hence the irony of it all: someone takes away your land and leaves a little for you—and then tells you to move because the land is too small for you!" (Nicholas 1991a).

Loss of Livelihood

> *Why give us seeds and fertilizers, if you give us no right to the land we work? We have planted the land before with dusun ["fruit orchard"] and rubber without any help from anybody. But the land we have worked has been taken arbitrarily by outsiders. We don't want to plant again for others.*
>
> Semai leader Bah Johan bin Din (Quoted in Todd 1990:9)

Loss of land obviously means loss of livelihood for any agricultural people, whether swiddeners, agroforesters, cashcroppers, or irrigated rice growers. It is incomprehensible to most Orang Asli that the JHEOA continues to urge foragers to become farmers and farmers to invest more resources and labor in planting cash crops when the Department cannot guarantee their rights to land or crops. "Lack of land security works directly against declared Government policy, which is to settle Orang Asli in one place, practicing modern cash-crop agriculture" (Todd 1990:12).

Loss of forest to logging or development has equally devastating effects on Orang Asli economies. Foragers like the Batek depend on wild tubers, fruit, game, and fish for their basic nutrition. Even agricultural groups use the forest as their main source of animal protein. Although farmers may grow a wide variety of crops, their animal husbandry is usually limited to raising a few chickens and goats. All Orang Asli with access to forest obtain most of their meat by hunting, which is why the JHEOA uses the blowpipe as a symbol for the Orang Asli as a whole. In addition, whether foraging or farming, Orang Asli depend on the forest for building and craft materials: poles, bamboo, and thatch for houses; pandanus for mats; and so on. Loss of those raw materials means substitutes must be bought, creating further demands on their meager cash incomes.

Loss of forests also removes a major source of cash income for Orang Asli. Logging and forest clearing for development often destroy Orang Asli fruit and rubber trees. If the owners receive any compensation at all, it is far less than the income they could expect to obtain from the trees over their productive lifetimes. For agroforesters like the west Semai, their trees are capital equipment: a major labor investment and their primary source of income. For almost all Orang Asli collecting and trading forest products—particularly rattan and *gaharu* wood—has been a crucial supplement to their incomes over the last few decades. On the basis of a detailed study of the role of rattan trading in Orang Asli economies, Hood Salleh and Ruth Kiew conclude that

> it is difficult to foresee how the orang asli could maintain a debt-free economy without rattan collecting, and the collecting of other minor forest products.... Without rattan-collecting the standard of living can be expected to drop below subsistence level and result in malnutrition of children. (1990:37)

> As one Orang Hulu [Jakun] said: "Habis rotan, habis orang asli" (no rattan, no orang asli), by which he meant that without rattan collecting the orang asli would become dependent on the government and would thereby lose their identity and culture. (1990:18)

Rattan has still not been successfully cultivated on a commercial basis in Malaysia; both rattan and gaharu wood are wild resources which depend on rainforests for their existence. As the forests disappear, then, so do these sources of Orang Asli income.

The Creation of a Rural Proletariat

> *Loggers have chopped down our durian and petai trees. We want the jungle to be left as it is. We prefer to live near the jungle as we have no skills to work outside the settlement. We don't like to be estate [plantation] labourers because we have been cheated of our wages in the past.*

Moreover, we don't like to work for others. We like to be free and live off the jungle. We don't fight among ourselves over the trees because we can identify which tree belongs to whom.

> Penghulu Yen of Sungai Bersih (Quoted in Man and Hoh 1987)

The effect of constant relocation, of outside parties seizing Orang Asli land and destroying Orang Asli capital in the form of trees, is to leave a rural population without a subsistence base. If the displaced people have no area to which they can move and rebuild their economies, their dispossession works like the enclosure acts in eighteenth century England: it creates a rural proletariat of people who must depend on paid work to survive. Without land, trees, or forest products, the only thing they have to sell is their labor.

Orang Asli have few job options. "With their limited education and skills they are generally engaged in the lowest of the menial jobs with little prospect for job improvement or job satisfaction" (Mohd Tap 1990:471-472). For most Semai, the "alternative to being arboriculturalists is not being dentists and lawyers, but being night watchmen, paramilitary police, day laborers, pieceworkers or prostitutes" (Dentan and Ong 1995:86-87). The most readily available jobs for Orang Asli as a whole are in the very industries that displaced them: logging and plantations (Mohd Tap 1990:471). They usually work on a contract basis or as pieceworkers rather than as salaried employees. Thus, their employment is sporadic, unreliable, and often takes the workers far from home. They have no control over the conditions of employment—they must take what they can get—and they are often cheated out of some or all of their earnings. Getting jobs as plantation workers, the worst paid steady jobs in Malaysia, is in fact a step up from being occasional laborers, since no one is worse off than they. The *Malay Mail* newspaper praised the plantation giant Kumpulan Guthrie for giving jobs to Jah Hut instead of to illegal Indonesian immigrants (Nichols 1991e). But Jah Hut used to have a profitable wood-carving industry.

Orang Asli forced to take menial jobs on plantations may show an increase in cash income, which government researchers cite as proof that the destruction of their traditional economies actually benefits them (Lim Hin Fui 1993). But any study of the transformation of self-sufficient and independent people into wage laborers can demonstrate an improvement by focusing solely on wage income. The picture is not so rosy if it takes account of the loss of productive capital (e.g., fruit trees); loss of income from that capital; loss of access to free materials from the forest; loss of health due to pollution and introduced diseases; and increased costs involved in wage work, such as transportation and equipment costs.

Orang Asli have become proletarians even in the collection of forest products. Forestry Department regulations require licenses for people to gather forest products. The licenses are generally too expensive for Orang Asli to obtain, so they usually go to non-Asli businessmen with good connections. Orang Asli who want to collect forest products must sell them to the license-holder, at prices he determines, instead of offering them to the highest bidder. Thus the licensing system transforms Orang Asli from independent entrepreneurs to dependent part-time pieceworkers, even in Orang Asli reserves.

Are the Orang Asli on the road to becoming "lumpenproletarians"—powerless, unskilled, occasional workers scrounging a living on the fringes of Malaysian society? In 1990 Endicott was sitting with some Batek in a coffee shop in Kuala Krai, Kelantan, when he was spotted by a man from a small Mendriq settlement on the nearby Taku River. That group had been employed for several decades as laborers on a rubber plantation, clearing weeds and maintaining paths. They had supplemented their wages by selling herbal medicines from the forest, but that source of income dried up with the clearing of the forest. In the late 1980s they became increasingly dependent on the JHEOA for economic assistance. The Mendriq man approached Endicott and asked him for a handout. The Batek were astonished and embarrassed. After Endicott gave the Mendriq man some money and he left, one Batek man remarked in disbelief, "He has no shame." Semai used to say that, if you went to the cities, you would see Malay, Chinese, and Tamil beggars, but never Orang Asli beggars, "because we look after our people." Apparently this is no longer true. Are more Orang Asli destined to become beggars like this unfortunate Mendriq man?

Development or Internal Colonialism?

> Developed sections . . . —in the capitol and on the coast—are a curious sort of imperialist power, having internal colonies, as it were.
>
> C. Wright Mills (1967:154)

Colonial powers take control of the land, resources, and labor of a subject people and extract the wealth generated for their own benefit. The subjects have no say in the arrangement. There are many continuities between British colonial policies in Malaya and the current government's development policies in Orang Asli areas. Even the land laws used to dispossess the Orang Asli are inherited from the British. Ideally development, unlike colonization, happens with the consent or on the initiative of the people most affected, and it directly benefits them. In Peninsular Malaysia, however, much development is a type of "internal colonialism" in which the government and powerful groups of outsiders colonize the Orang Asli.[3] It involves transferring wealth from the Orang Asli, the poorest members of Malaysian society, to developers, who are some of the richest.

Contrary to the claims of some government officials, Orang Asli are not against development. The Semai who held logs hostage in Pahang wanted development (a road, piped water, electricity), not money. The Temuan in Negri Sembilan who applied for a license to log their reserve wanted to use the profits to invest in rubber and durian orchards. Left to their own devices, Orang Asli welcome development, provided that it is on their terms and meets at least some of their needs. Time and again, without outside help, in response to market opportunities, they have adopted economic activities which integrate them into the Malaysian economic mainstream more effectively than any government program could (see, e.g., Gomes 1986). In short, Orang Asli are only against development which is against them. So far development has harmed Orang Asli more than it has helped them.

---

3. See Hind 1984 for details of the concept of "internal colonialism."

5

Regroupment and Islamization:

The Government's Solution to the "Orang Asli Problem"

The Orang Asli present a two-fold problem for the Malaysian government: they are a hindrance to development and a political embarrassment. Its proposed solution to the problem combines "regroupment"—settling Orang Asli in concentrated settlements—and "Islamization"—converting them to Islam, so they can be absorbed into the Malay population.[1]

REGROUPMENT

During British rule, the resettlement schemes which were implemented were successful in that the short-term objectives were achieved.

---

1. For further information on the effects of government programs on Orang Asli, see McLellan 1983; Rohini Talalla 1984; Means 1985-1986; Endicott 1987; Mohd Tap 1990; Nicholas 1994; Howell 1995; Dentan and Ong 1995. Mohd Tap's Ph.D. dissertation (1990) is a detailed critical analysis of the work of the JHEOA based on his fieldwork and thirteen years of experience as a senior officer in the Department.

However, the department felt that to integrate the Orang Asli with society the socio-economic standing of the people had to be improved and this could only be done by bringing development to them. . . .

Under the regroupment schemes, the Orang Asli are taken from one location to another but they are still in their hereditary areas.

> Baharon Azhar bin Raffie'i, former Director-General of the JHEOA (Quoted in *New Sunday Times* 1983)

If they want to resettle us, it's OK if it's done . . . with houses, crops, and other facilities. But they resettle us and just give us a few houses and nothing else. What do the authorities think we are—dolls? furniture? That we do not need a livelihood to survive? That we do not need water, electricity and roads?

> Jakun from Pahang (Quoted in *Pernloi Gah* 1993:4)

Introduction

In 1974 and 1975, the vestigial Communist Party of Malaya, perhaps encouraged by the Communist successes in Vietnam, launched some terrorist attacks against public monuments and trains. Their military stronghold was in the central mountains on both sides of the Thai border, an area inhabited by Temiar, Jahai, and Lanoh. In 1977 the National Security Council, fearing that the Orang Asli would once again fall under Communist control, ordered the JHEOA to move the Orang Asli out of that area (Jimin et al. 1983:48-54; Mohd Tap 1990:280-282; Nicholas 1990:69-70). The Department's policy at the time was to avoid resettling Orang Asli, because it had had such disastrous consequences when the military did it in 1952-1953 (Carey 1976:320 n.11; Jimin et al. 1983:50), but it could not reject such an order. So the Department made a counterproposal that the Orang Asli not be removed but merely "regrouped" in consolidated settlements within or near the people's traditional areas. Department officials argued that the military could monitor the Orang Asli in regroupment areas, and the Department could institute economic modernization on a larger scale than before, thus serving two purposes at once. The government accepted this proposal.

Regroupment was started to facilitate surveillance and control. But it soon became the Department's basic method for "developing" Orang Asli economies everywhere. During the 1960s and early 1970s the JHEOA had tried, with little success, to introduce cash-cropping (especially rubber production) into communities which did not already do it, a process termed "in situ land development." The Department saw regroupment schemes (*Rancangan Perkumpulan Semula,* "RPS") as an opportunity to modernize Orang Asli economies by fully integrating them into the national market economy. It therefore extended the use of regroupment schemes "outside the security sensitive areas with a view of providing a comprehensive development package to overcome the slow progress of the improvement approach [in situ land development]" used on fringe groups since the early 1960s (Mohd Tap 1990:282-283). The Department especially targeted foragers, swiddeners, and groups displaced by dams.

The Plan

The JHEOA modeled Orang Asli regroupment schemes after an early form of FELDA scheme designed to provide family farms for landless Malays (Mohd Tap 1990:87, 285; see Chapter 4). Orang Asli regroupment schemes are intended to be relatively self-contained communities with an administrative center surrounded by family farms and communal plots of forest and pasture land for grazing livestock. The Department supplies access roads, a school and dormitory, a medical clinic, a cooperative shop, an administrative and management office, a combination multipurpose hall and Muslim chapel, and some houses. Each family should get ten acres of land for rubber, oil palm, and fruit trees, and two acres for a house and subsistence crops (Jimin et al. 1983:96; see *New Straits Times* 1982b for slightly different figures).

Although the emphasis on individual family plots, rather than communal property, is borrowed from Malay practices, there are two important differences between Orang Asli regroupment schemes and FELDA schemes. Orang Asli do not have to pay back the cost of developing the land, as Malays do. But Orang Asli, unlike Malays, can never own the land allocated to them.

The overall plan, which was to begin in 1979 and continue until 1994, envisioned up to thirty-seven regroupment schemes containing about 25,000 people (roughly one-third of the Orang Asli population at the time) and costing about US$100 million (Jimin et al. 1983:95-96; *New Straits Times* 1982b; Nicholas 1990:70). The last regroupment scheme was implemented in Johore in 1995.

The Appeal of Regroupment Schemes to Planners

Regroupment not only promises to solve some of the practical problems of ensuring national security and integrating the Orang Asli into the national economy, it also satisfies some deeply rooted Malay ideas about what is the proper way for Orang Asli to live.

Sedentization

One advantage of regroupment in the eyes of officials is that it settles Orang Asli down in one place. To ruling class Malays the value of settling them down is self-evident. It needs no justification. Since the 1950s the JHEOA has tried to get foragers to become farmers and swiddeners to take up permanent field agriculture, often for no obvious reason. These programs do open up land to non-Asli, make administration and control more convenient for the JHEOA, and so on. But it would be unfair to think that these are the only considerations involved. The JHEOA also sees itself as bringing civilized order out of unkempt wandering.

The Malay ruling class has a powerful dislike for people who are "free" (Malay *bebas*). Unlike the English term "free," the connotations of Malay *bebas* are negative. To be *bebas* is to be irresponsible, licentious, and lacking in civilized restraint. Malay court favorites who could flout the law, Chinese secret societies which defied it, and the great Perak Malay chiefs who were immune from taxes were all *bebas*. Conservative lowland Semai refer to their highland kin and the Temiar as *bebas,* with a sneer. To ruling class Malays, *bebas* Orang Asli are something to be deplored, like the "wild Indians" of American mythology.

To Malays the surest sign that Orang Asli are *bebas* is that they "wander about" in the jungle. To educated Malays, the English term "nomadic" has many of the same negative connotations as *bebas.* In the Malay view of Orang Asli, even farming groups are "nomadic." To Malays the complex patterns of movement required by foraging or swiddening seem random and senseless. Even former Director-General Jimin bin Idris claims that before about 1960 most Orang Asli "simply roamed all over the place" (quoted in Todd 1990:12). Apparently it is the *bebas* nature of their movement that is so irksome, not movement per se. The occupationally dictated movements of loggers, school teachers, and even government bureaucrats are not cast in a negative light.

Political Control

One major JHEOA goal is to bring the Orang Asli under government control. Officials learned during the Emergency how dangerous it is to national security for a segment of the population to be autonomous. Although the threat of Communist subversion has diminished, the government's desire to control the Orang Asli has not. Its zeal in this respect must be understood partly in terms of Malay political traditions. In Malay kingdoms everyone except the ruler was under someone else's authority. The egalitarian relations so often seen among Orang Asli did not exist. Rulers saw people outside the political hierarchy as threatening to proper social order. In the Malay feudal hierarchy the proper place of Orang Asli was as subjects, if not slaves. Today the patron-client relationship between the JHEOA and the Orang Asli continues the traditional hierarchical relationship which ruling class Malays feel is the proper order of things.

In regroupment schemes the JHEOA can exercise greater control over Orang Asli than when they are living in their own villages or camps. The Department has found that its own staff, even Orang Asli, have little authority in the eyes of Orang Asli. Therefore, it has tried to incorporate Orang Asli political systems into its own bureaucracy. Among groups which traditionally had leaders, such as the Temuan *batin*, the people's hereditary or chosen leader is officially recognized and is paid a small salary. The Department reserves the right to accept or reject the people's choice of leader. The leader is then expected to act as liaison, conveying his group's concerns to the Department and organizing and motivating the people to carry out the Department's wishes. Among groups without a traditional political hierarchy, like the Batek and east Semai, the Department either appoints headmen (called *penghulu* or *batin*), as sultans and chiefs did in the past, or urges the group to choose one, a choice the Department can accept or reject. Department officials, used to Malay hierarchy, express great frustration with the inability of Orang Asli leaders to control their followers, even in groups that traditionally had leaders. But apparently this policy of "indirect rule" works better than trying to rule directly through Department employees posted in Orang Asli settlements.

Economic Modernization

As mentioned above, another JHEOA goal is to "modernize" Orang Asli economies. The Department wants to shift the emphasis from subsistence activities to activities directed toward market exchange—selling commodities or labor and buying food and other necessities. It considers it a sign of economic progress when a group abandons subsistence farming (Jimin et al. 1983:196). In regroupment schemes the Department can easily introduce the economic changes it desires, because the traditional economy is destroyed.

Officials do not explain *why* Orang Asli economies should be modernized in this way, believing, perhaps, that the advantages are self-evident. Colonial governments often force colonized people to give up subsistence production in order to generate trade which the rulers can monopolize and tax. Such a rationale hardly applies in the Orang Asli case, however, for the amount of profit or tax revenue their commercial activities might generate would be tiny. The argument that the Orang Asli would be better off as part of the market economy hardly applies either. As we will show, the modernization of Orang Asli economies over the last three decades has been correlated with a *decline* in their standard of living. The reason for the policy probably lies in the general belief among Malaysian policy-makers that sedentization and economic development are inherently good. Officials consider traditional Orang Asli subsistence activities backward and shameful, while they see market-oriented ones as "progressive" and "modern." As a former Deputy Prime Minister said, the Government's programs for Orang Asli are to ensure that they are not "left behind in development that would improve their way of life" (*New Sunday Times* 1986).

Regroupment in Practice

Implementation

Except in security areas, the authorities do not force people to join regroupment schemes. Officials do talk up the numerous modern conveniences that the Department will supply, even implying that everyone will get prefabricated houses. They take leaders to see similar projects already in operation. They promise to provide the infrastructure and all the equipment, seedlings, and fertilizers necessary for planting and tending the crops, along with food and financial assistance until the cash-crops begin to produce income. One attractive feature of regroupment schemes, especially to groups that have experienced encroachment on their traditional territories, is the perception that there is some security of land tenure. Officials lead people to believe that if they do not like living in the regroupment scheme, they have the option of returning to their original area, which was indeed true in the early days of the regroupment program (see, e.g., Nicholas 1990:85 n.9; 1994).

In truth, however, regroupment is a one-way street, because after Orang Asli leave, outsiders usually log off their land and take it over for their own purposes (Nicholas 1990:80; Todd 1990:11-12). Often outsiders take over the land first, displacing the Orang Asli. Only after their entire home area had been logged off and converted into oil palm and rubber plantations did any of the Batek De' of Kelantan consent to settling at the regroupment center at Pos Lebir.

The JHEOA was well aware that regroupment would only work if all the infrastructure and support systems were in place before the people were relocated, since they would have no other resources to fall back on at the regroupment site. The plan was that

> Orang Asli would only move into the new areas upon the completion of the construction of dwelling houses for each family, the availability of all social service facilities (health, education and personal welfare), and the completion of the first stage of the agricultural project [clearing the land]. Food rations, and monetary help would be given during the whole gestation period of rubber and other cash crops grown. (Jimin et al. 1983:169-170)

In practice, however, difficulties delayed completion of the facilities, leading to Orang Asli being rushed into regroupment schemes that were not yet ready. For example, the Department depends upon loggers to deforest the land, but in northeastern Perak and northwestern Kelantan depressed timber prices and security restrictions on access to the area halted logging for some years. In two areas, Dala and Kemar, some of the proposed area was cleared, but the JHEOA failed to supply the promised tree crops. In Banun, near the Thai border, 800 Orang Asli were cut off when the rising waters of the Temenggor dam flooded the access road. The failure to anticipate the flooding is odd, since the regroupment was to accommodate the dam.

Cash allowances offered in the initial years before the crops matured—for example, in the Betau Regroupment Scheme in Pahang—were inadequate to support the families (Nicholas 1990:72).

> For a household of two adults and four children, the monthly allowance of $50-00 [US$20] would be exhausted within two weeks on the purchase, for example, of 10 kg of milled rice, 2 kg of sugar, 5 cans of sardines, and quantities of cooking oil and kerosene. Also, with friends and relatives frequently making

> house-visits, the allowances were grossly inadequate to cover the costs of entertaining them. (Nicholas 1990:85 n.13)

Men who happened to be away when the JHEOA officers arrived to dispense the subsidies sometimes were simply not paid (Harjit Singh 1983).

Land

The JHEOA has been quite successful in getting states to designate land as Orang Asli reserves for regroupment schemes, probably because the areas are small and officials can claim that regroupment promotes national security. But regroupment areas, like American Indian reservations, are on land that has been rejected by other communities (Mohd Tap 1990:46).

> Even the choice of land to be "declared" Orang Asli reserves or areas is, first and foremost, dependent on the land not being considered "commercially important" by the authorities. Land given out to Orang Asli is usually considered "second class land", that is, land with poor soil quality, inadequate irrigation and poor infrastructure, physically situated in remote areas and unattractive to the other communities. Above all, the land is devoid of any commercially viable resources like timber and minerals. More often than not, the resources would be extracted before these areas are "handed over" to the community. As a result, the land given out to the Orang Asli needs to be "well rehabilitated" before it could be used for agriculture. (Mohd Tap 1990:69-70)

In short, most regroupment areas begin as wastelands.

Another characteristic of the land provided in regroupment schemes is that it is always much smaller than the area the regrouped people originally inhabited and used. For example, the area allocated to Semai at the Betau RPS in Pahang was only 15 percent of the size of the people's original territory (Nicholas 1990:71-72).

Economic Programs

The JHEOA goal in regroupment schemes is to foster cash-crop arboriculture. The favored crop is rubber, though the price of rubber is generally low and subject to wild variations depending on world market demand. Probably the Department continues to favor rubber because it requires little skill to grow and process, needs minimal equipment, and fits Departmental expertise. The Department has also encouraged people in some regroupment schemes to grow oil palm, coconut, coffee, and commercial fruits, and to raise cattle.

Oddly enough, after trashing traditional Orang Asli subsistence activities, the Department has promoted growing fruits and vegetables for home consumption and sale in some regroupment schemes, as part of the national "Green Earth Program" (*Ranchangan Bumi Hijau*), the Malaysian version of the "green revolution" (Nicholas 1990:74, 85 n.16; Mohd Tap 1990:505). Apparently the government considers this kind of subsistence farming desirable because it is imposed by government planners, not initiated by the people themselves, and therefore is "progressive."

> The programme became successful and created surpluses among communities that participated, but the programme did not include the provision for marketing. The Orang Asli ended up with agricultural surpluses which could not be consumed locally while at the same time they could not be marketed outside the village. (Mohd Tap 1990:505)

Innovations that looked good to planners in Kuala Lumpur often proved unworkable on the ground. For example, the JHEOA decided to provide cattle to some regroupment schemes where the forest had been degraded to grassland, so that Orang Asli could sell meat, milk, and excess animals as the herds grew (Nicholas 1990:73). In one instance, the Department delivered cows by helicopter to Semai in Tenau, Perak, without considering that, if the cows could come in only by helicopter, meat and milk could come out only in the same way. The result was that the Semai, who feared killing the cows and did not know how to milk them (even if milk had been part of their diet), had to build fences to keep the useless animals from eating their fields and befouling their settlement (Gomes 1987). The basic economic problem with the regroupment schemes is that the assistance given in the early years and the income generated by the cash-crops later are inadequate to support the residents. They are forced therefore to fend for themselves, seeking whatever sources of food and income they can find, and consequently neglecting their cash-crops. Typically they are "compelled to divert some of their time and energy into production activities geared towards exchange" (Nicholas 1990:72). The re-grouped Semai in Pahang concentrate on gathering *petai* beans in their old home areas and searching for rattan in any remaining patches of rainforest they can find (Nicholas 1990:73). Temiar at RPS Betis were reduced to selling frogs to Chinese businessmen for income (Rose 1993).

Housing

One of the attractions to Orang Asli of the regroupment schemes is the plank houses the JHEOA supplies. People want the houses, they say, because (1) they are a trade-off for giving up their traditional lands, and (2) they look like Malay houses and thus signify that the inhabitants are not poor and despicable. Orang Asli are sensitive to the earmarks of their poverty.

The Department has developed a standard house, a small version of a type of rural Malay house. It is a rectangular structure on short posts with a verandah at the front, one or two living/sleeping rooms, and a kitchen at the back. It is prefabricated from wooden timbers and planks and has corrugated metal or asbestos-cement roofing. The Department does not modify the plan to suit local conditions, cultures, or wishes. Some features of the standard house are undesirable for any group, such as the roof, which makes the house unbearably hot when it is sunny and rattles violently during rainstorms. "It is a common feature for recipients of these houses to construct a traditional house for daily living, alongside or attached to the pre-fabricated house supplied. In such circumstances, the modern house is generally used for storage and for show to visitors" (Mohd Tap 1990:90).

Another problem is that, instead of providing houses for all settlers as promised, the Department usually provides only a few, which it designates for the "headman" and other prominent individuals. Others have to improvise, using bought materials or scarce materials from the regroupment area. Sometimes leaders turned down houses offered them because they were uncomfortable with the resentment caused by being elevated above the rest of the group (Hasan Mat Nor 1993).

Education

The JHEOA provides school buildings and, until recently, teachers for regroupment schemes. Most JHEOA schools cover only grades 1-3, after which children must go to boarding schools. Schools are usually housed in prefabricated buildings with plank walls, corrugated metal roofs, and wire mesh on the windows. Central primary schools (grades 1-5) also have dormitories for students from outside the immediate area. Until recently teachers in the smaller schools were JHEOA field staff—Malays and a few Orang Asli. They were not trained teachers, and most had a low level of education themselves. Teachers in the central primary schools were Malays from the Ministry of Education, usually those who did poorly on their exams and thus could not get more desirable postings.

The JHEOA's educational program was—all parties admit—a dismal failure (Carey 1976:301, 333; Jimin et al. 1983:70; Mohd Tap 1990:260-270; Juli Edo 1991). On average a quarter of the children who started primary school dropped out in the first year (Mohd Tap 1990:263). About 70 percent of all students dropped out by the end of grade five (Mohd Tap 1990:265, 270). This means less than 30 percent of Orang Asli (including those born before education was available) are functionally literate according to UNESCO standards and therefore able to qualify for jobs in the modern sector (Mohd Tap 1990:265). As of 1984, no graduate of JHEOA schools had ever gone beyond secondary school; "the tiny handful of Orang Asli who [had] made it to tertiary level education were all products of State schools" (*New Straits Times* 1984). Recognizing the failure of its educational program, the JHEOA turned over responsibility for education to the Ministry of Education in 1995.

Medical Care

The JHEOA has provided medical care to Orang Asli since the Emergency, when its field assistants at jungle forts began dispensing simple remedies. The hub of the system was (and still is) the 450-bed Orang Asli hospital at Gombak, in a forested valley twelve miles outside Kuala Lumpur. The hospital also serves as a training center where Orang Asli take courses like house-building and midwifery. The mixing of people from different groups at the hospital has fostered a sense of Orang Asli identity.

Each regroupment scheme has a clinic of a size appropriate to the population served. A typical clinic is a partially prefabricated building containing an examination area, a few patient beds, a medicine storage area, a two-way radio set-up, and a living area for the medical assistant. Most clinics also have a helicopter landing pad. Medical assistants ("paramedics"), some of them Orang Asli trained at the Orang Asli hospital, serve on two-month rotations. They are responsible for looking after minor medical problems, educating the local people on health and hygiene, and radioing for the helicopter whenever a seriously ill patient needs to be evacuated. A medical officer, a doctor, makes tours of the clinics every month or so.

The quality of the medical care provided is mediocre, and Orang Asli suffer from numerous health and nutritional problems (*New Sunday Times* 1983; Khor 1985; Hurst 1990:55; POASM 1991:26-28; Jeyakumar Devaraj 1993:11-12). The standards and practices of the 1950s and 1960s were commendable for the time, but they have not improved. Many medical assistants are poorly trained, motivated, and supervised. As a former JHEOA Director-General said, some spend more time fishing than treating their patients. Some doctors, showing the typical educated Malay's dislike for being away from the comforts of the city, are reluctant to go to rural and forest areas, so the number of visits to outlying clinics has fallen. Most Orang Asli near towns now seek medical care at government clinics instead of JHEOA facilities.

Other Facilities

The JHEOA provides each regroupment scheme with an access road, a multipurpose hall including a Muslim chapel, an administrative office, housing for staff, and a simple provisions shop offering food, tobacco, tools, cloth, trinkets, and so on. Often, however, the roads are inadequate, and electricity and water supplies are lacking, even when they are provided to adjacent Malay settlements (POASM 1991:13).

The JHEOA has also provided outhouses to some settlements. One Semai headman came back disgusted from a meeting in 1992 at which government officials promised to build latrines for a group of Semai villages. His assessment:

> What we need here is housing, housing and electricity. What they give us is houses for shit. We need houses for ourselves, not for our shit.... They didn't ask us what we wanted.... Maybe I should hang my mosquito net in the shit house and sleep there [laughs]. What a joke!

Some Cases of Regroupment

RPS Betau

The Betau regroupment scheme lies in the eastern foothills of the Main (Titiwangsa) Range of mountains about thirty-eight miles north of Raub, Pahang, where the Jelai River joins the Betau River (Ong Hock Chuan 1984; Hasan Mat Nor 1989; *Sunday Star* 1993; Nicholas 1994). It is one of the largest regroupment schemes, containing 1356 east Semai on 2860 acres. Settlements occupy 572 acres; another 572 acres are devoted to fruit trees; and 1716 acres are rubber and palm oil plantations. The only connection with the outside world is an unimproved logging road to the FELDA settlement of Sungai Koyan about eleven miles away (*Sunday Star* 1993).

There are twenty settlements in the scheme, each containing a group of families from a common hereditary area in the upper reaches of nearby rivers. The settlements are beside the rivers, surrounded by rubber trees, gardens, and orchards. About two-thirds of the settlements contain some plank houses, but not enough to house all resident families. So traditional bamboo and thatch houses are common as well. The settlements are connected by dirt roads which are impassable when it rains.

The scheme headquarters is at Fort Betau. "The Betau administrative complex includes office blocks and guest houses, a six-classroom school (from kindergarten level until primary three), a cooperative store, a coffee-shop, staff quarters, students' hostel, community hall, surau and a hospital. All . . . are basically timber with asbestos roofing" (Nicholas 1994:18). There is also a library and dining hall associated with the school complex. The clinic should be manned by a trained nurse, a laboratory assistant, and an ambulance driver. It has basic medical facilities. Severe cases are rushed to Raub (Ong Hock Chuan 1984).

Thirteen years after RPS Betau opened, a Malay anthropologist who had originally supported the plan reported abandoned houses, a "hospital" with no medical staff, and unhappy people.

> Ideally, RPS should be self-sufficient, creating a conducive environment for the Semais to take part in the country's economic activities. . . . Their lifestyle should have changed tremendously—for the better. I am sad that this scheme did not turn out as planned. The land cultivated with rubber trees [was] supposed to generate income for them but Felcra [Federal Land Consolidation and Rehabilitation Authority] has taken over instead. (Hasan Mat Nor, quoted in Matayun 1993; see also Hasan Mat Nor 1989)

The Semai at Betau were unfamiliar with rubber agroforestry, and in thirteen years no one taught them how to process rubber (Hasan Mat Nor, quoted in Rose 1993). A Temiar rubber plantation at RPS Betis failed for the same reason. Felcra, which took over tapping the trees, was supposed to pay the people dividends for their rubber, but so far the single dividend to arrive (in 1990) was for $M28 (a little over US $10) per family (Rose 1993).

Pos Lebir

Pos Lebir, on the Lebir River about twenty-five miles south of Kuala Krai, Kelantan, is the focus of a regroupment area for Batek and other Semang from the Lebir River valley. In 1971 the post consisted of a school, playing field, medical hut, helicopter pad, and houses for the schoolteacher and a field assistant, all surrounded by rainforest. The only access from the outside world was by helicopter or outboard motorboat. A few families were settled at the post, living mainly by swiddening. The vast majority of the Batek were still forager-traders living in the upper reaches of the Lebir watershed.

In 1990 the post looked much the same except that it was bordered by a grove of weed-infested rubber trees with scrub forest—the aftermath of logging—on the hills beyond. A dirt (laterite) road passed the post, connecting it to a highway downstream and to an endless series of oil palm and rubber plantations upstream. The only new buildings were two more houses for staff, an unused Muslim chapel, and two plank houses, one for the headman and the other for his nephew. Professional staff included a medical assistant, a field assistant, and a schoolteacher who was seldom there. The other permanent residents, seventeen families, lived in tiny wood and bamboo huts surrounded by tapioca and banana plants. The residents eked out a living by tapping their rubber trees and occasionally working for the JHEOA or logging companies. A wooden building housed a diesel generator, but it was not operating because the people could not afford the small monthly fee for electricity. A gas-powered pump beside the prayer hall was meant to supply river-water for ablutions, but it was broken. The short-wave radio in the medical hut did not work either. The grass on the playing field was knee-high because the Orang Asli maintenance man had died six months before, and the Department had not hired a replacement.

Department officials in the state capital of Kota Bharu explained the neglect and decrepitude of the post by saying that they were reluctant to invest more money in it because the state government was threatening to build a dam a few miles below the post which would flood the entire lower valley.

They had not told the Batek, however, and were still pressuring them to settle at the post and the adjacent village of Kampung Macang.

A number of Batek had tried living at Kampung Macang during the 1980s, but found they could not make a decent living tapping rubber. They were also put off by the Department's attempts to convert them to Islam and uncomfortable being exposed to uninvited visits by curious outsiders. They preferred to live in the surviving fringe of rainforest at the edge of the National Park and trade rattan and *gaharu* wood.

Many Batek refused even to try living at the regroupment scheme. As one man told Endicott in 1981, "I will never settle at the post. If you want to find me the next time you come, you will find me in the forest in the headwaters." Several hundred Batek have now retreated deep inside the National Park (Taman Negara), where they are "hiding" from the outside world. In the park they have been able to carry on their own religious rituals and maintain a semblance of their preferred foraging and trading way of life.

But life there is not without its difficulties. The increased population in the park has depleted the wild food sources. Park rangers try to stop them from collecting and trading forest products, which are also becoming scarce. Aggressive Thai *gaharu* wood poachers, who illegally cross into Malaysia, harass them and compete with them for the remaining *gaharu* wood. Bangladeshi workers from oil palm plantations in Kelantan have raped and killed some Batek women. The police cannot protect them. The JHEOA and the Department of Parks and Wildlife, which is in charge of the National Park, both ignore them, each expecting the other to take responsibility for them. Still, for all the difficulties, they choose to live in the forest, as their deities meant them to, rather than participate in the dubious benefits of regroupment and development.

Sungai Rual

The Sungai Rual regroupment scheme is located about five miles west of the small town of Jeli in the northwest corner of Kelantan. It contains 1630 acres of land, which were gazetted as aboriginal reserve in 1991. The inhabitants are Semang, former foragers. Most are Jahai, but some are Mendriq, and there are a few Batek. They come from seven bands which originally inhabited the area within a thirty-six mile radius of Jeli. Now numbering about 280, they live in four hamlets located at different points along the Rual River, which passes through the reserve.

The JHEOA provided the usual facilities, including a school and a clinic. Between 1972 and 1988 about sixty-four hectares were planted with rubber trees, forty-seven hectares with fruit trees, and several more with home gardens. A further twenty hectares were set aside as grazing land for the cattle provided by the government.

Because the Rual people resisted settling down at the reserve, the Department had to entice them with free handouts of food. Families were given rations while their cash-crops were maturing, and children received food if they went to school. The people became increasingly dependent on these handouts. Whenever supplies of food were not forthcoming, they would stop working on the projects and set out into the forest to forage and collect rattan. The consequent inconsistency of their agricultural work caused some of the projects to fail. For example, in 1975 a rice cultivation project yielded only enough rice to feed the people for one week. The poor harvest was due to their not adequately weeding the fields or guarding the crop against pests. In 1978, the people threatened to uproot the young rubber trees they had planted if their request for food rations was not met immediately. Their threats and "foot-dragging" can best be understood as acts of resistance to the whole concept of regroupment.

Now, however, the Rual people no longer have their traditional areas (*saka*) to return to. Economic development of the region, largely facilitated by the construction of the East-West Highway, attracted many Malay migrants, who quickly laid claim to the land and the valuable fruit trees once owned by the Semang. The state government also opened their *saka* to logging. There were numerous conflicts between the Malays, loggers, and Semang over land. Being a powerless minority, the Semang lost out most of the time. Without forest resources to fall back on, they now have no choice but to live in the regroupment scheme and grow cash-crops.

Life as cash-croppers is not easy for the Rual Semang. Because of the low price of rubber, they are struggling to make enough money to pay for food and other necessities. Without access to wild foods and with too little time and land to grow subsistence crops, their diet has deteriorated, causing malnutrition. Living crowded together in unsanitary conditions has led to an increase in communicable diseases like dysentery and cholera. The mortality rate has risen, and people now have more children to compensate.

Poverty and the loss of their traditional areas have profoundly demoralized the Rual people. Their *saka* were sources not just of food, but of group identity. Stories of the past are rooted in the landscape of their *saka*. Regroupment has robbed them of their identity and history as well as their economic security.

Now they are in danger of losing the little land they have left. The Rual people had long been plagued by outsiders harassing and exploiting them and stealing timber, rattan, and fruit from inside the reserve. Repeated complaints to the JHEOA and the District Office brought no action. In early 1993 cholera broke out in one of the hamlets, killing half a dozen people (Nicholas 1993). The JHEOA responded by removing them from the area until the outbreak died down. While they were gone, Malay settlers began to clear the land and plant fruit trees to establish their ownership.

On April 25, after the Semang had returned, a Malay man entered the settlement and told the people that he had bought the land (Nicholas 1993). He ordered them to leave at once. When they refused on the grounds that the land was a gazetted aboriginal reserve, he called them names, including "Sakai," and threatened to return the next day with some friends to evict them.

The next morning five middle-aged Malays entered the hamlet in a van. Two of them brandished machetes, loudly ordering the Semang to leave. The intruders threatened and insulted the people. One Malay kicked the elderly headman to the ground. A nineteen-year-old boy rushed to his aid and was cut on the arm by another Malay. Suddenly a brawl broke out. When the dust settled one Malay was dead, apparently beaten to death. Two others who fled died later, allegedly from poisoned darts. Eventually nine Semang men were arrested and charged with manslaughter. After several adjournments, the court case is still going on at the time of this writing.

This tragic event shows the Rual people's high level of anxiety, frustration, and desperation. Orang Asli are well known for fleeing from confrontation, but the Semang of the Rual regroupment scheme have nowhere left to run.

Results of Regroupment

Poverty and Insecurity

On the whole the government's economic programs both inside and outside of regroupment schemes have failed to benefit Orang Asli. Most Orang Asli are actually worse off now than they were before the government began its efforts to "develop" their economies. JHEOA Director-General Hassan Ishak concedes that Orang Asli are the poorest Malaysians, making about M$2100 (US$830) annually by government estimates (as opposed to the average income of M$7600). About 80 percent of Orang Asli, he adds, are *termiskin*, the "poorest of the poor" (quoted in Matayun 1993; see also Todd 1990:12; Mohd Tap 1990:328, 471-472).

Besides being poor, regrouped Orang Asli are vulnerable to fluctuations in commodity prices. Neither they nor the JHEOA can anticipate what crops will command good prices five years down the line, when trees start to produce. Even with mature trees, producers experience incomprehensible cycles of boom and bust as demand fluctuates, but the needs of their families are constant. Even in good times the price of rubber—the JHEOA's favored crop—is low. Small-scale rubber farmers ("smallholders") of all ethnic groups are one of the poorest segments of the Malaysian population. As one critic of the JHEOA economic program says, making Orang Asli into rubber smallholders moves them from one poverty sector to another (Nicholas 1990:76, 85 n.18).

The shift toward dependence on the market economy also makes Orang Asli vulnerable to being exploited by middlemen. The JHEOA does not adequately protect them from exploitation; in some cases the exploiters are Department employees (Mohd Tap 1990:84). The Department's control over trade at regroupment schemes has actually made matters worse by restricting the number of middlemen the Orang Asli can deal with.

> In the Betau Regroupment Scheme in 1984 only one individual was authorized to enter the scheme and trade with the Semai of the twenty settlements therein. Because of the monopsonistic nature of the relationship, he was able to offer (and get) prices for rattan and petai which were 20 to 50 percent lower than what was being offered in other similar non-scheme areas. (Nicholas 1990:85 n.19)

Dependency

One unintended consequence of regroupment and the associated displacement of Orang Asli from their land has been their dependence on the government for survival. In the Semai case, with

> their ability to be self-subsistent and self-reliant being drastically impaired, the Semai have been forced to seek government aid in almost every sphere of development. Consequently, in place of traditional self-confidence, the Semai were reduced to a state of "imitative dependence." This is a highly degraded state associated not only with an inability to provide themselves adequately with the material means of sustenance but also with the loss of cultural and psychological integrity. (Nicholas 1990:78)

Since World War II, "the Orang Asli have been transformed to a community that is totally dependent on the Department [JHEOA] and the government for even the most trivial of things, like buying pencils for their school going children" (Mohd Tap 1990:486).

The patron-client relationship which the JHEOA maintains with the Orang Asli also contributes to the Orang Asli's "imitative dependence" mentality. Ideally good recipients of government largesse should work hard to get off welfare as soon as possible. But good clients (in the feudal sense) should be dependent on and grateful to their benefactors. Thus the JHEOA's patronizing practices create the very dependency it officially deplores (Gomes 1987).

The dependence of Orang Asli at regroupment schemes makes it easy for government officials to blame Orang Asli for the failure of the programs. They are said to be "against development," lazy, and ungrateful for all the government has done for them (*New Straits Times* 1988a; Mohd Tap 1990:497; POASM 1991:12-13). Blaming Orang Asli "attitudes" for the failure of government programs—in which they have had no say—arises from and reinforces negative stereotypes of Orang Asli. As a secret policeman once complained to Dentan, "We [Malays] have given them everything, and still they want to live in the jungle." This of course overlooks the fact that before the government "gave" them the regroupment areas, it *took away* their traditional homelands and independent livelihood.

"Successes"

Although regroupment has failed to turn Orang Asli into independent commercial farmers, it has achieved other government goals. It has succeeded in removing the Orang Asli from their land, which is coveted by other groups and interests (Nicholas 1990:76).[2]

> Felda and other land agencies have cleared huge tracts of jungle in which Orang Asli used to harvest *rotan* [rattan] and durian. Now major highways planned to cross the main range will open up the last undisturbed areas, and both Government and private companies are eyeing opportunities for mining, cattle-farming and plantations. (Todd 1990:11)

No doubt this result, at least as much as the desire to bring Orang Asli into the mainstream, explains why the govern-

---

2. Similarly, American President Andrew Jackson had the "Civilized Nations" of Native Americans (Chocktaw, Cherokee, Chickasaw, and Creek) "relocated" from the American Southeast to Oklahoma—defying a Supreme Court decision—to allow developers access to their lands (Anders 1979).

ment has persisted with regroupment, at considerable expense to itself, long after the security threat which gave rise to the regroupment program has ceased to exist.

Regroupment has also accomplished some of the JHEOA's specific goals. It has helped to "modernize" the Orang Asli economies by eliminating swiddening and most other subsistence activities, while totally integrating them into the market economy (Nicholas 1990:71-73, 75-77). Residents of regroupment schemes must now buy almost all the necessities of life, even building and handicraft materials they once obtained for nothing from the forest. It has also assisted assimilation by breaking down features of traditional Orang Asli cultures which are incompatible with Malay practices. These include such things as egalitarian social and political relations, economic equality, communal land ownership, traditional religious beliefs and practices, and even Orang Asli languages. Finally, it has tightened the government's political control over the Orang Asli (Nicholas 1990:74, 77; Mohd Tap 1990:286, 485-490). The Department uses the authority granted by the Aboriginal Peoples Act to ensure that only leaders acceptable to itself are confirmed. In addition, in regroupment schemes the Department introduces various specialized agents—including project managers, schoolteachers, and medical assistants—who have authority in their own sphere of expertise. In summary, as a former JHEOA Director-General says,

> There is no doubt that the efforts of the Department have brought a lot of changes among the Orang Asli. The value system, and general norms of the Orang Asli have obviously changed. . . . It is also quite obvious that the traditional sociopolitical organization of the Orang Asli has been affected. As a result of their exposure to outside forces, brought about by "governmental interest", the traditional organizational structure of the community has, to a certain degree disintegrated. (Jimin et al. 1983:135)

Social Problems

Relocation and the breakdown of traditional social organization and norms at regroupment schemes and other exposed settlements have had a number of unfortunate consequences. One is the loss of traditional knowledge. For example, young Semai in fringe villages no longer know the names and properties of rainforest plants (Dentan and Ong 1995:56). But their schooling is so poor that they have not learned any scientific botany either. In this connection, young people have lost respect for the knowledge of elders, because it is not relevant to the modern world. People now turn for advice to educated teachers and paramedics rather than to traditional leaders and shamans (Mohd Tap 1990:488-489).

Alcohol abuse has become a problem in a number of rural settlements (Mohd Tap 1990:492-493). Heavy drinking is often associated with all-night dancing (Malay *joget*) parties, sometimes with hired bands playing Malay-style rock. These parties may represent "a form of protest against the regimentation of life of the younger generations" (Mohd Tap 1990:493). Drinking is also a blatant rejection of Islam and Malays, who consider imbibing alcohol a major sin (Mohd Tap 1990:494).

Although Orang Asli generally drink cheaper forms of alcoholic beverages (palm toddy and rice wine), alcohol consumption can be a significant drain on a family's budget (Mohd Tap 1990:492-493). Most heavy drinkers are men, although women are also beginning to get drunk. Men's drinking often leads to conflict with their wives. A Semai woman from Sungkai told Dentan that the only time she fought with her husband was when they had been drinking. Excessive drinking can also lead to death: between 1976 and 1991 seven men from the single Semai settlement of Mncak, population less than 200, died in vehicular accidents related to drunkenness.

Alcohol consumption is usually involved in the still rare—but increasingly frequent—incidents of violence in Orang Asli communities. In a survey of Semai violence in 1991-1992, Dentan found that acts of violence almost always arose from all-night drinking parties. Typically, as the party wears on, one or more drunken outsiders begin to molest the young Semai women. Then drunken young Semai men intervene, and fighting erupts. Usually cooler heads manage to calm down the combatants, but sometimes the fighting goes on until someone gets seriously hurt.

Prostitution has become common at some settlements and regroupment schemes where substantial numbers of male outsiders are present, such as RPS Betis in Kelantan and RPS Betau in Pahang (Hasan Mat Nor 1989). Malays voice astonishment at the sexual freedom of Orang Asli women. "Orang Asli men just can't control their women," says a Malay paramilitary police officer disdainfully. In fact, for Orang Asli in the hills, marriage did not confer a sexual monopoly, and the idea that one person could control another's sex life seemed ridiculous. People got jealous, of course, and bartering sex for trinkets from a Malay or Chinese trader seemed tacky to some people, but such barter was fairly rare and posed no social problem. Nowadays some Orang Asli women do make a business of prostitution, however. A few Orang Asli women and transvestite men have even taken up prostitution in the cities (Tan Chee Khoon 1980; *New Straits Times* 1988e).

Male outsiders, especially those in positions of authority, molest and sexually harass Orang Asli women with impunity. This creates intense resentment (Mohd Tap 1990:153), but Orang Asli men are more or less helpless to defend the women against more powerful outsiders. The line between consensual sex, prostitution, and rape is fuzzy under these circumstances. An outsider who takes an Orang Asli woman by force may simply pay a small fine to the village headman. To the offender the fine is merely the price of the sex (Hasan Mat Noor 1989).

These social problems are dishearteningly familiar to students of marginalized indigenous peoples. Similar problems afflict Native Americans and Australian Aborigines, for example. Their causes are complex and related to the people's particular circumstances, but they have something in common. As Mohd Tap concludes for Orang Asli, drinking, dancing, and gambling seem to be expressions of their frustration and "inability to fulfill their expectations of the 'good life'" (1990:495).

ISLAMIZATION PROGRAM

> *Political memories usually run short but even as we make our commitment today on alleviating the lot of the indigenous people, it would only be honest to recall the horrible deeds of the past inflicted on thousands and thousands of indigenous people, especially in the Americas [,] in the name of so-called civilisation and religion.*
>
> Tan Sri Razali Ismail, Malaysia's permanent UN representative in a speech marking the beginning of the International Year of the World's Indigenous Peoples (Oh 1993)

> *In an era of fanaticism, invasions were made upon them [Orang Asli] with the object of converting them to Mohammedism but the only result was fire and bloodshed and after each conflict the surviving Sakais fled further into the forest (into those parts which had never been before explored) or to the natural strongholds of the far off mountains.*
>
> G. B. Cerruti (1908:109)

Introduction

As we explained in Chapter 3, the government's ultimate goal is to absorb the Orang Asli into the Malay population. Officials do everything they can bureaucratically to expunge the idea that Orang Asli differ from Malays. In all censuses since 1970, they submerge Orang Asli population figures in the Malay category (Means 1985-1986:638). In government statistics Orang Asli appear only as "Malay" and *bumiputera*. On government forms there is no Orang Asli ethnic category; "when it comes to filling government forms, most Orang Asli face a dilemma as to whether to tick 'Malay' or 'Others'" (Nicholas 1991a:2). Recently UMNO, the dominant Malay political party, has accepted Orang Asli members, even though membership is technically restricted to Malays.

The exhibits on Orang Asli cultures which once had a prominent place in the National Museum (Muzium Negara) have now been removed to the obscurity of a small museum at the Orang Asli hospital at Gombak, twelve miles outside Kuala Lumpur. Government tourist brochures do not mention them. Most tourists now will never know that Orang Asli exist.

The JHEOA also tries to keep Orang Asli away from non-Malays, especially Chinese, who might influence them to remain separate from the Malays. For example, when newspapers published an account of how some Chinese doctors had volunteered their services on weekends to a couple of Semai settlements, the Malay ruling class responded angrily (Albela 1992).[3] The JHEOA denounced the visits as illegal, since they took place without Departmental permission. Malay officials made a well-publicized visit to the site, distributing medicines. The matter then vanished from public view. The medical attention also ceased. When JHEOA officials interfere with contacts between Orang Asli and Chinese today, they justify their actions by saying the Chinese are Communists, even though most are fully engaged in private enterprise (e.g., as loggers or traders).

After the surrender of the last Communist guerrillas in 1989, the government appropriately transferred the JHEOA from the Ministry of Home Affairs, which is responsible for national security, to the Ministry of Rural Development. But in 1993 it moved the Department to the new Ministry of National Unity and Social Development (Nicholas 1994:115 n.4), signaling a renewed emphasis on assimilation.

What remains to be done is to induce the Orang Asli actually to "become" Malays. This transformation requires, above all else, converting them to Islam.

Methods

Until the mid 1970s the JHEOA concentrated on "mainstreaming" Orang Asli by raising their living standard. Although the Department allowed Muslim religious organizations and individuals—including schoolteachers and Department officials—to proselytize Orang Asli, it did not

---

3. The fact that it took a newspaper story to inform the JHEOA of regular visits that had been going on for a couple of years shows how little the Department knows about conditions in Orang Asli settlements.

give them official backing. But in the late 1970s the government began to pressure the Department to actively promote Islam among Orang Asli (Mohd Tap 1990:228; see Chapter 3).

The JHEOA therefore formed a special *dakwah* ("Islamic propagation") unit to proselytize Orang Asli and to coordinate the activities of other Muslim missionary groups (Mohd Tap 1990:229, 462–463). The staff are Muslim Orang Asli with special training in missionary work. They use persuasion only, trying to convince other Orang Asli of the virtues of the Muslim beliefs and lifestyle.

In the early 1980s, JHEOA officials developed an ambitious master plan for converting all Orang Asli to Islam (JHEOA 1983). The JHEOA was to provide general support and coordinate the activities of other agencies. One part of the plan called for religious facilities and instructors to be provided to all Orang Asli communities. For example, at Pos Lebir the Kelantan state Religious Affairs Department built a Muslim chapel (*surau*) and hired a religious teacher to lead voluntary religious classes among the Batek living at the post. He commuted by motorbike from the Malay village of Kampung Lalok. Since few Batek were interested, he usually went home shortly after he arrived. According to the plan, less accessible groups were to receive occasional visits from members of missionary groups, who would lecture, preach, and sometimes show films.

Another part of the plan was aimed at creating a visible distinction in prosperity between converts and non-converts—a process called "positive discrimination"—in order to give Orang Asli a material incentive to convert. The Department tried to provide converts with better housing (including water and electricity supplies), income-earning opportunities, schooling, health, and transportation facilities than it supplied to non-Muslims. It also provided converts with religious equipment, such as prayer mats and wall clocks, and gave them allowances for the expenses of Muslim holidays. (Some non-Muslim families also received supplies for Muslim festivals, in less generous amounts, presumably as an incentive for them to participate.) The Trengganu Department of Religion gave motorbikes to some Batek converts. In addition, the JHEOA gave preference to Muslim

Orang Asli employees in promotion decisions; it is generally understood that a non-Muslim cannot rise to the upper ranks in the Department. Muslim employees of the Department were also to get special rewards for converting other Orang Asli.

The planners were well aware that Orang Asli would only convert if they felt that Malays would accept them into their community as equals, something they have not readily done in the past (JHEOA 1983:7; Mohd Tap 1990:7, 338-343, 400-404, 441-449). For example, shortly after World War II, the Trengganu Department of Religion convinced some Batek to adopt Islam and settle near a Malay village. Some even learned to read the Quran. Before long, some Malay men married Batek women. But when a Batek man announced his intention to marry a Malay woman, the Malays were out-raged, and the Department of Religion forbade it. The disillu-sioned Batek later abandoned their settlement and renounced their Muslim identity.

The master plan therefore called for educating Malays, es-pecially those living near Orang Asli communities, to induce them to accept Orang Asli converts into the brotherhood of Islam. Malays were to be taught more about Orang Asli, and there were to be monthly sermons in the mosques on the topic of "toleration toward Orang Asli" (JHEOA 1983:23). The government sometimes stages elaborate parties for con-verts, often followed by "integration" ceremonies at a mosque between converted Orang Asli and local Malays, marking their official assimilation (Chan Siew Wah 1987). Converted Semai showed Dentan photographs of themselves shaking hands with the Prime Minister at such a ceremony. The Islamic Center (*Pusat Islam*) in the Prime Minister's De-partment has sponsored some Orang Asli converts' minor pilgrimages to Mecca (*umrah*) in appreciation of their contri-bution towards the development of Islam in their community (Nicholas 1992b:17, citing *Berita Harian*, November 25, 1992).

In a 1989 meeting with officials from the Islamic Affairs Division of the Prime Minister's Department, the Institute for Proselytization and Islamic Training, and the Centre for Is-lamic Studies, a JHEOA official said that "Orang Asli school teachers should be oriented so that in addition to teaching

Orang Asli children, they also conduct Islamization activities among the Orang Asli communities" (JHEOA 1989). He also advocated programs to convert students living in school hostels. But the Aboriginal Peoples Act prohibits giving religious training to any Orang Asli child without the parent's or guardian's prior consent.

The Department's goal of converting Orang Asli to Islam also requires keeping them from adopting other religions. The JHEOA skirts the Constitutional guarantee of religious freedom by using powers set out in the Aboriginal Peoples Act to exclude Christian missionaries from Orang Asli communities. In 1981 the Department even banned two Christian Semai from the Semai-run Misi Metodis (Methodist Mission) in Perak from visiting "pagan" Semai settlements in Pahang, on the dubious grounds that the latter area "belonged to Islam."

At first the JHEOA pursued the goal of Islamizing Orang Asli more or less covertly (JHEOA 1983:12). The Department recognized that the Islamization program was open to question on legal and ethical grounds (Mohd Tap 1990:450) and that it might draw criticism from non-Malays. Department officials did not even admit publicly that the program existed, and its budget was buried in that of the Division of Research and Information. But recently the government has begun to publicize the program (see, e.g., *Berita Harian* 1993; *The Star* 1995b). Apparently UMNO politicians now feel that the advantages of letting Malay voters know about their efforts to convert Orang Asli override the disadvantages of possibly being called to account for them by jurists or opposition politicians.

By 1993 government agencies had built 265 combination multipurpose halls and religious schools in Orang Asli settlements at a cost of M$20 million (about US$8 million) (*Berita Harian* 1993). The buildings typically are two-story structures with a community hall on the ground floor and a Muslim chapel on the upper floor. According to a Deputy Minister in the Prime Minister's Department, the federal government will build a total of 300 such structures in Orang Asli settlements around the country (*Pernloi Gah* 1993:4, citing *New Straits Times*, January 13, 1993). The government intends to place religious officers in all these facilities to "guide the Orang Asli toward embracing Islam" (*Berita Harian* 1993).

Most Semai with whom Dentan talked said they were happy to get any facilities, but those provided had nothing to do with their most pressing needs: safe water, electricity, roads, housing, and so on. The headman of one Semai settlement complained to the JHEOA that what his people wanted was an improved access road and a bridge. The community hall would be useful, he said, but he could see no use for the chapel, since his people were not Muslims (Nicholas 1991b:3). Dr. Abdul Hamid Othman, Deputy Minister in the Prime Minister's Department, disagreed. He said providing religious facilities "was part of the Government's community service to bring development to the Orang Asli in line with the United Nations' International Year for the World's Indigenous Peoples." Aside from religious facilities, he said, "there was not much Malaysia needed to do to improve the infrastructure for Orang Asli settlements as such facilities had been made available a long time ago" (*Pernloi Gah* 1993:4, citing *New Straits Times*, January 13, 1993).

Results

How successful, then, has the government's Islamization program been? Before looking at the statistics, we must briefly consider what counts as success. All that is needed for Orang Asli to be listed as Muslims is for them to have made the declaration "There is no God but Allah and Muhammad is His prophet." Many "converts" are Muslims in name only. They do not believe or even understand Islamic doctrine, and they follow few if any Muslim practices. Some, after making the declaration in a moment of enthusiasm or weakness, "revert" entirely to their traditional behavior, although according to Malaysian law a Muslim can never cease to be a Muslim. Census takers may list anyone who does not object—and Orang Asli are easily intimidated—as Muslims. JHEOA staff have every incentive to overreport their success in converting Orang Asli. Therefore, the government's published figures on the numbers of Orang Asli Muslims must be viewed as optimistic.

With that in mind, the results of the government's twen-ty-five-year-long Islamization program are not impressive. According to JHEOA figures, about 3 percent of Orang Asli—mostly Orang Kuala—were Muslims before the government's Islamization program began (Carey 1976:234-235). In 1993, the figure given by a government official was only 10 percent, making the total 8,000 Muslims out of an Orang Asli population of 80,000 (*Berita Harian* 1993).

What accounts for the slow progress of the Islamization program? Orang Asli voice a number of objections to becoming Muslims, centering mostly on ritual requirements rather than spiritual ones. One major sticking point is the requirement that Muslims be circumcised. A Semai nickname for Malays is "the chopped people," referring to circumcision. The idea of chopping off flesh is repugnant to most Orang Asli. In fact, the Perak Religious Affairs Department, which has had the most success in making converts, does not require circumcision for Orang Asli converts (*New Straits Times* 1983). Of non-Muslim Orang Asli, only Semelai and some Jakun and Jah Hut practice circumcision.

Orang Asli also often mention food restrictions as a reason for rejecting conversion. Orang Asli diet is extremely varied. It includes many species of plants and animals Malays shun, some of which are subject to Islamic food tabus. Traditional Semai, like Batek, insist that they could not survive if they gave up the foods conversion would require. Certainly the loss of wild game especially, without substitute sources of animal protein, would lead to nutritional deficiencies. Orang Asli living close to Malay settlements, however, often do not eat foods offensive to their Malay neighbors, apparently to avoid Malay criticism. West Semai insist, however, that these dietary restrictions—which may be part of the reason for the general malnourishment of rural Orang Asli—are individual idiosyncrasies and that following Malay tabus would be impossible. Fasting all day, as good Muslims must do during Ramadan, would also be very difficult for them, they say.

On a theological plane, Islam seems alien and incomprehensible to many Orang Asli. Although Muslim missionaries ignore this fact, most Orang Asli groups have full-blown religions of their own, which make sense of their world and give meaning to their lives. Their beliefs, prohibitions, and rituals are intricately woven into their everyday lives. As one Batek man told Endicott, "We can't just forget our deities."

It does not help their case that many Muslim missionaries show little respect for the Orang Asli and present their own religion in a dogmatic and self-righteous manner. Unlike their Christian counterparts, Muslim missionaries seldom venture into the backcountry where most Orang Asli live, and they never actually live with those they hope to convert, preferring instead to make brief visits to them (Chan Siew Wah 1987). Among the most zealous proselytizers are those espousing a form of Islam based on Arabic culture, even to the extent of wearing long, hot Arab-style robes. Most Orang Asli fail to see the sense of adopting such a doctrine and life-style (Mohd Tap 1990:456).

Perhaps the major underlying reason Orang Asli resist adopting Islam, however, is that they simply do not want to "become Malays." Most Orang Asli prefer to live among their own people, and they derive a sense of security from being part of their community and kinship network. On the other hand, they do not generally like Malays and have no desire to associate more closely with them. Orang Asli who convert to Islam often find themselves cut off from their own people, but not fully accepted by their Malay co-religionists (Mohd Tap 1990:226, 453). They cannot even eat with other Orang Asli because of Muslim food prohibitions. To convert to Islam, then, is to step into the abyss between two societies, a drastic step indeed.

Many Orang Asli actively resist Islamization. When Endicott asked one Batek man why he and his family had fled from the regroupment scheme at Pos Lebir, he answered with a single word: "Islam." Batek resent the fact that only Orang Asli, and not Chinese and Indians, are expected to become Muslims. Some Orang Asli have become Christians and Bahai to escape the pressure to convert to Islam (Mohd Tap 1990:457). Although the government tries to keep non-Muslim missionaries away from Orang Asli, at least 1500 Orang Asli had become Christians by 1984 (*Malay Mail* 1984). Most are Semai, overwhelmingly concentrated in Perak. After Bahai missionaries traveled through Malaysia in the mid

1970s, over 300 Orang Asli adopted the Bahai religion (Carey 1976:325, 329; *Malay Mail* 1984), but Professor Juli Edo, a Semai anthropologist at Universiti Malaya, says that the number of Bahai had diminished to a very few by the mid 1990s.

The Malaysian government's Islamization program has not only largely failed to achieve its goal, it has caused great resentment toward the government and the JHEOA in particular. Orang Asli resist joining regroupment schemes in part because doing so exposes them to relentless pressure to become Malays. Taking government employment, such as joining the army or the Senoi Praak, does too. As a former JHEOA officer says, "the efforts to propagate Islam do little to increase interaction and integration of Orang Asli and their Malay neighbors, but rather have contributed to the increase in tension between the two communities" (Mohd Tap 1990:455).

Converting Orang Asli to Islam also raises a serious legal problem which advocates of Islamization have not addressed. As Muslims, Orang Asli converts would be subject to the states' *syariah* legislation, but, as Orang Asli, they are restricted by the Aboriginal Peoples Act (Hooker 1976:172-185). Orang Asli cannot be subject to two conflicting sets of laws. If appreciable numbers of Orang Asli ever do become Muslims, the government will have to repeal the Aboriginal Peoples Act.

In early 1995, JHEOA Director-General Hassan Ishak admitted at a meeting with Orang Asli Association leaders that the Department's Islamization program was a "bad idea." But it is unlikely that the JHEOA will be allowed to return to its former policy of integration (without assimilation) because of political pressures from above.

6

The Future of the Orang Asli

The Orang Asli of the future will enjoy their full place in the Malaysian sun, while retaining their special position as the truly indigenous inhabitants of this country.
Former JHEOA Director-General Iskandar Carey
(1976:336)

WHO SPEAKS FOR THE ORANG ASLI?

Orang Asli should speak out more and inform us as to what they prefer to do. . . . The government is willing to learn from its mistakes.
Datuk Khalid Ismail, Secretary-General of the Ministry of Culture, Arts and Tourism (Quoted in Shaila Koshy 1993)

Leadership

Being administered by a single agency and called by a single term for forty years has created a sense of unity among Orang Asli (Carey 1976:335), much as the notion of being "Native Americans" emerged among the indigenous peoples of North America. This developed especially through their interactions at the Orang Asli hospital at Gombak, where they met and mingled as patients and staff and in training programs. They also feel a common bond as poor people and subjects of discrimination (Dentan 1992). But Orang Asli have been slow to become politically organized and to develop a voice in Malaysian life. Even tribal peoples like the Kayapo of Brazil have achieved greater recognition and clout in national and international affairs.

One reason is that the Aboriginal Peoples Act has enabled the JHEOA to exercise enormous control over Orang Asli. The JHEOA's top-down planning procedure and the absence of Orang Asli in policy-making positions leaves no avenue for Orang Asli to voice, let alone act on, their concerns. The Department coopts Orang Asli leaders by making them minor functionaries in the bureaucracy. It has been able to nip any signs of independent political activity in the bud. The Department's deliberate "'breaking up' of the traditional leadership structure has been used to 'short-circuit' troublesome leaders in the community. The much favoured *modus operandi* is the promotion of well-known but sympathetic (to the Department) individuals" (Mohd Tap 1990:449 n.4). Until the mid-1970s the Constitutionally mandated Senator "capable of representing the interests of aborigines" (Article 45[2]) was a Malay (Carey 1976:149). He is said to have never spoken a word during his long tenure in the Senate.

Another major reason Orang Asli have been slow to develop an independent organization and voice is the poor quality of their education. Orang Asli do not know their rights or how to exercise them. Lack of formal education handicaps potential leaders like the Semai Bah Sudeew, who has been active in Orang Asli affairs for thirty years. Even an exceptionally intelligent and forceful leader like Tanyogn, the Batek's female "headman," cannot emerge as a spokesperson in a sophisticated society like Malaysia without educational qualifications. Some Orang Asli say that the JHEOA deliberately uses incompetent teachers for fear that Orang Asli will become independent. They cannot believe that the JHEOA educational system can be as bad as it is by accident.

Lack of a secure land base is a political disadvantage as well. Unlike Native Americans, Orang Asli have no sovereignty over their reserves. There is no longer any place in which they have political control.

Despite these obstacles, a few well-educated Orang Asli leaders have emerged in recent years. Some are current or former JHEOA employees, especially in the medical section, who have gained skills and sophistication through on-the-job training. Some have succeeded by adopting the government's stance and outlook. Others, like Itam Wali, the Aboriginal Senator since 1984, balance support for official policies with sympathy for the concerns of Orang Asli themselves. For instance, he has campaigned hard—unsuccessfully so far—to have the Constitution amended to include Orang Asli as one of the categories of people with special privileges (Juhaidi Yean Abdullah 1995).

Other leaders have risen outside the JHEOA. They are mainly west Semai, Jakun, and Semelai from rural areas where they have been able to attend regular government schools rather than those run by the JHEOA. A few have even obtained university degrees. They include Bah Tony Williams-Hunt—the Semai son of the first Federal Advisor on Aborigines, P. D. R. Williams-Hunt. Bah Tony, who obtained a degree in economics at Universiti Malaya, works as a banker and is active in COAC and the Perak branch of POASM (see below). When he applied for a job with the JHEOA shortly after getting his degree, he was turned down (Abdul Jalil Hamid 1989). Several Orang Asli have obtained master's degrees in the Department of Anthropology and Sociology at Universiti Kebangsaan Malaysia, under the tutelage of Professors Hood Salleh, Hasan Mat Nor, and their colleagues. One graduate of the program, Juli Edo, is a lecturer in anthropology at Universiti Malaya, now doing a Ph.D. at The Australian National University.

Organizations

POASM

In 1977 some Orang Asli employees of the JHEOA incorporated the *Persatuan Orang Asli Semenanjung Malaysia* ("Association of Orang Asli of Peninsular Malaysia") or POASM as an organization to represent their interests. Membership is open to all Orang Asli and *bumiputera* over age sixteen for an enrollment fee of M$1 and annual dues of M$1. The founders were JHEOA employees, but by the end of the 1980s it had about 2000 members from throughout the Peninsula.

The activities and stance of POASM have fluctuated, reflecting the differing orientations of its leaders. The first president—Itam Wali, then a JHEOA employee—emphasized cooperation with the Department in pursuing its goals. At first POASM concerned itself mainly with the "airing of petty grievances, especially on behalf of Orang Asli Departmental personnel" (Mohd Tap 1990:500 n.11). After Itam Wali became Senator, POASM elected Bah Tony, a JHEOA outsider, as president. He took a more independent line, sometimes critical of the Department. Under his leadership POASM began campaigning for Orang Asli rights through the media and through meetings with government officials. This shift upset JHEOA officials. Bah Tony opted not to run for president again in 1991, although he was still popular with members. In his absence, Long Jidin, a Jakun veterinarian who had the support of the JHEOA, was elected. His first action was to invite all high JHEOA officials to join and to ask the Director-General to serve as official advisor, thus restoring the familiar paternalistic relationship with Malays. Soon after, the government allocated M$33,000 (US$13,200) to POASM. Not surprisingly POASM became compliant to government wishes again.

Whether POASM will be an independent voice for Orang Asli in future depends on whether the JHEOA can continue to coopt its leaders. Rivalries continue between members who support government policies wholeheartedly and those who are more critical. As long as membership is open to all Orang Asli and all members have a vote in elections, POASM has the potential to be an independent avenue for Orang Asli aspirations and actions.

COAC

A small multi-ethnic group of Malaysian volunteers, including some Orang Asli, founded the Center for Orang Asli Concerns (Malay *Pusat Prihatinan Orang Asli*) or COAC in 1989. COAC encourages and facilitates the development of independent community and regional Orang Asli organizations. Its most active members include Colin Nicholas, a researcher on Semai economic change, Bah Tony, and Bah Sudeew. It publishes an occasional newsletter, *Pernloi Gah* (Semai for "Bearing the News") in Malay and English editions. The newsletter features current events affecting Orang Asli (usually compiled from an assiduous reading of the Malay- and English-language newspapers) along with interviews with Orang Asli and other miscellaneous material. COAC also organized a group of volunteer lawyers to defend the Pos Rual Semang who were accused of killing three Malay intruders (see Chapter 5), when JHEOA officials tried to get the defendants to plead guilty.

COAC generally reflects the views of independent educated Orang Asli. It often criticizes policies of the government and of the JHEOA in particular. In response some pro-government officials criticize it. For example, Long Jidin, while president of POASM, accused COAC of being controlled and financed by foreign anthropologists and NGOs (non-governmental organizations). The Malaysian government regards NGOs—even Malaysian ones—with deep suspicion, because they sometimes question or criticize government policies. Groups supporting such causes as environmental protection and human rights must tread very carefully. In 1987 the government arrested a large number of government critics under the Internal Security Act, including Harrison Ngau Laing, a Kayan activist from Sarawak (*Asiaweek* 1995). But Long Jidin's charges against COAC went too far. COAC sued him for libel, and he settled out of court. COAC also sued the newspapers that printed his charges, and that case is still ongoing.

ORANG ASLI ASPIRATIONS

As Orang Asli leaders knowledgeable about laws and the workings of government have emerged, they have begun to express what they want the government to do for their community. Despite some differences of opinion, their basic concerns are essentially the same. In 1991 Senator Itam Wali headed a twelve-member working group, including prominent Orang Asli intellectuals and POASM representatives, which drew up a plan titled "Development for Orang Asli in the Context of Vision 2020" (POASM 1991).[1] The following is an abbreviated summary of the main proposals.[2]

- The Federal Constitution is to be amended to include extension to the Orang Asli the rights accorded to the Malays and the indigenous peoples of Sabah and Sarawak under Article 153.

- Act 134 is to be reviewed so as to cater for the contemporary needs and aspirations of the Orang Asli. A committee, with Orang Asli forming the majority, is to be formed to undertake the review. Amongst others, provisions that must be incorporated into the Act are those that guarantee recognition of Orang Asli rights to their land, Orang Asli rights to self-determination and Orang Asli rights to practise their traditional culture and ways of life.

- Orang Asli rights to their land are to be recognised. Such rights are to be incorporated into Act 134 and the National Land Code or in a new legislation created for this purpose. In addition to this, gazetting of, and granting titles to, Orang Asli land are to be carried out by the Authorities immediately.

- Orang Asli economic development is to be stepped up and this task is to be entrusted to all the relevant Government agencies. . . . The approach taken must be one that emphasises the solving of Orang Asli structural problems, involvement of Orang Asli in the planning and implementation processes, and development that is based on the wants and needs of the Orang Asli.

- Infrastructure like roads, electricity and water supply are to be provided to Orang Asli villages.

- A more comprehensive educational development programme is to be introduced for the Orang Asli. Such programme should include rendering Orang Asli with

---

1. Vision 2020 is the Prime Minister's plan for making Malaysia a fully industrialized and developed country by the year 2020.
2. Translated by Bah Tony Williams-Hunt, a member of the working group (Williams-Hunt 1992:5-6).

all the necessary assistance, facilities and incentives, including assuring a certain number of places for them in institutions of higher learning. The quality of educational services provided to the Orang Asli should be upgraded, and towards this end, the administration of JHEOA-run schools must be taken over by the Ministry of Education. . . .

- The standard of health services rendered to the Orang Asli is to be further improved. . . . The JHEOA hospital at Gombak is to be taken over by the Health Ministry, but its status is to remain as an Orang Asli hospital. . . .

- Orang Asli culture is to be recognised as part of the national culture. Orang Asli traditional rules and laws are to be accorded recognition like that given to the Native Customary Laws of the indigenous people of Sabah and Sarawak. A public holiday is also to be declared for the Orang Asli. Orang Asli freedom to practise any religion, including their own indigenous religions, is to be recognised.

- Orang Asli are to be given the opportunity to participate in politics. Such involvement is to be through representation in Parliament and in the State Executive Councils.

The main thrust of these recommendations is that Orang Asli want development and integration into mainstream society, but with their ethnic identities intact. In many ways the recommendations recall the Statement of Policy of 1961, which was abandoned in part after the government adopted the assimilation policy. These recommendations also echo those in the "Memorandum" that came from a conference of twenty-seven Orang Asli headmen from numerous groups in 1982 (Means 1985-1986:649-652; *New Straits Times* 1982a). The headmen distributed copies of their Memorandum to the press and every member of Parliament, but never received an official response from the government. The recommendations address the concerns of both leaders and ordinary Orang Asli, like their fear of losing their land. So far the only recommendation that has been enacted is the request that the

Education Ministry take over responsibility for Orang Asli education.

To enact these recommendations, the government would have to amend the Constitution and revise the Aboriginal Peoples Act and the National Land Code. Amending the Constitution to extend special rights to Orang Asli would fulfill the government's moral obligation to the country's "original people" and would contribute far more to alleviating their poverty than the JHEOA's failed development programs. Orang Asli and other concerned people have been calling for revisions to Act 134 for many years (*The Star* 1982; *New Straits Times* 1990). Some Orang Asli even want the Act repealed, since the conditions that made it necessary in 1954 no longer exist. As recently as 1992, however, government officials refused to make any changes, claiming that the law has never impeded Orang Asli development (*The Star* 1992a). But in May 1994 scholars at the Universiti Kebangsaan Malaysia organized a forum—including Orang Asli, academics, legal experts, and government officials—to consider what changes are needed. Participants formed a task force to draft revisions to the Act and the Constitution (Edwin 1994a, 1994b). As of the time of this writing (November 1995), they have not yet issued their report. And whether the government will act on it is an open question.

Orang Asli are divided on what the future of the JHEOA should be (Means 1985-1986:651; Edwin 1994b). Some want it continued but put under Orang Asli control. Others want it abolished or replaced by a different type of agency, arguing that it just separates them from the rest of society and duplicates, less effectively, the functions of other government agencies. Some say if Orang Asli were given the same privileges as Malays, there would be no need for the JHEOA.

The Orang Asli's vision of their future—integration as a distinct and respected community in Malaysia's ethnically diverse society—is different from the government's vision—assimilation into the Malay population. The one that prevails depends largely on the government, which has the power and resources to impose its will. Orang Asli can resist, but cannot affect the basic circumstances in which they live. But current government policies do not seem to be achieving their goal. They appear to be transforming the Orang Asli into a demoralized rural lumpenproletariat, rather than a contented subgroup of Malays. The government must decide if that is what it wishes to achieve. At present the prospects of Orang Asli achieving their goals appear bleak. The Malaysian government shows little indication that it is moving to change the legal status of Orang Asli. It remains to be seen whether humanitarian concern for the welfare of Orang Asli will override the political benefits the government hopes to derive from its current policies.

References

Abdul Jalil Hamid
  1989   "White" Asli Hopes Future Better for Community. Daily Express. February 22.

Abdullah bin Abdul Kadir
  1960   Hikayat Abdullah, vol. 2. Singapore: Malaya Publishing House.

Adi Haji Taha
  1985   The Re-excavation of the Rockshelter of Gua Cha, Ulu Kelantan, West Malaysia. Federation Museums Journal 30 (New Series):iii-134.

Aiken, S. R., and C. H. Leigh
  1992   Vanishing Rain Forests: The Ecological Transition in Malaysia. Oxford: Clarendon Press.

Albela, Geraldine
  1992   Doctors' Jungle Service. New Straits Times. May 19.

Ali M. A. Rachman
  1984   Energy Utilization and Social Structure: An Analysis of the Temuan Orang Asli of Peninsular Malaysia. Unpublished M.A. thesis, Universiti Malaya.
  1985   Organisasi Kerja dan Transformasi Sosial: Analisa Perbandingan Khasnya Mengenai Masyarakat Kubu dan Temuan di Semenanjung. Unpublished Ph.D. diss., Universiti Malaya.

Alper, Joe
  1993   How to Make the Forests of the World Pay Their Way. Science 260:1895-1896.

Andaya, B. W., and L. Y. Andaya
  1982   A History of Malaysia. London: Macmillan Education Ltd.

Anders, Gary
  1979   The Internal Colonization of Cherokee Native Americans. Development and Change 10:41-55.

Anderson, Benedict
1991   Imagined Communities: Reflections on the Origin and
        Spread of Nationalism. Revised edition. London and New
        York: Verso.

Anderson, John
1824   Political and Commercial Considerations Relative to the
        Malayan Peninsula and the British Settlements in the Straits
        of Malacca. Penang: William Cox for the Government.

APPEN
1990   Golf Courses in Malaysia: A Growing Problem. APPEN
        [Asia-Pacific People's Environmental Network] Features
        #19.

Arasaratnam, Sinnappah
1979   Indians in Malaysia and Singapore. Revised edition. Kuala
        Lumpur: Oxford University Press.

Asiaweek
1995   Much Done and More to Do: A Malaysian Activist Prepares
        His Next Move. Asiaweek. November 3:9.

Baharon Azhar bin Raffie'i
1973   Parit Gong: An Orang Asli Community in Transition. Un-
        published Ph.D. diss., University of Cambridge.
1986   The Temuans and the Wider Malaysian Society: Integration
        and Assimilation. In The Nascent Malaysian Society, second
        ed. Dahlan H. M., ed. Bangi: Universiti Kebangsaan Malay-
        sia.

Bellwood, Peter
1985   Prehistory of the Indo-Malaysian Archipelago. Sydney: Ac-
        ademic Press.

Benjamin, Geoffrey
1985   In the Long Term: Three Themes in Malayan Cultural Ecol-
        ogy. In Cultural Values and Human Ecology in Southeast
        Asia. Karl L. Hutterer, A. Terry Rambo, and George Love-
        lace, eds. Pp. 219-278. Ann Arbor: Center for South and
        Southeast Asian Studies.

Berita Harian
1993   265 Pegawai Agama Bimbing Orang Asli. Berita Harian.
        July 24.

Bulbeck, David
1985   The 1979 Gua Cha Skeletal Material. In The Re-excavation of
        the Rockshelter of Gua Cha, Ulu Kelantan, West Malaysia.
        Adi Haji Taha, ed. Federation Museums Journal 30 (New Se-
        ries):96-97.

Burger, Julian
1987   Report from the Frontier: The State of the World's Indige-
        nous Peoples. London and New Jersey: Zed Books.

Bury, J. B.
1932   The Idea of Progress: An Inquiry into Its Origin and Growth. London: Macmillan.

Carey, Iskandar
1976   Orang Asli: The Aboriginal Tribes of Peninsular Malaysia. Kuala Lumpur: Oxford University Press.

Cerruti, G. B.
1908   My Friends the Savages: Amongst the Sakais in the Malay Peninsula. Como, Italy: Tipografia Cooperativa Comense.

Chan Looi Tat
1991   The Originals. Asiaweek. September 6:46-53.

Chan Siew Wah
1987   Probe on Missionary Activities. The Star. October 10.

Chapman, F. Spencer
1957   The Jungle Is Neutral. London: Corgi Books.

Couillard, Marie-Andrée
1984   The Malays and the "Sakai": Some Comments on Their Social Relations in the Malay Peninsula. Kajian Malaysia 2(1):81-108.

Dentan, Robert Knox
1968   The Semai: A Nonviolent People of Malaya. New York: Holt, Rinehart and Winston.
1976   Identity and Ethnic Contact: Perak Malaysia 1963. Journal of Asian Affairs 1(1):79-86.
1992   The Rise, Maintenance, and Destruction of Peaceable Polity: A Preliminary Essay in Political Ecology. In Aggression and Peacefulness in Humans and Other Primates. J. Silverberg and J. P. Gray, eds. New York and Oxford: Oxford University Press.
1993   A Genial Form of Ethnicide. Daybreak. Autumn: 18-19, 13.
1995   Bad Day at Bukit Pekan. American Anthropologist 97:225-231.
In Press   The Persistence of Received Truth: How the Malaysian Ruling Class Constructs Orang Asli. In Politics, Land and Ethnicity in the Malay Peninsula and Borneo: Non-Malay Indigenous Groups and the State. R. L. Winzeler, ed. New Haven, Conn.: Yale Southeast Asian Studies Program.

Dentan, Robert K., and Ong Hean Chooi
1995   Stewards of the Green and Beautiful World: A Preliminary Report on Semai Arboriculture and Its Policy Implications. In Dimensions of Tradition and Development in Malaysia. Rokiah Talib and Tan Chee-Beng, eds. Petaling Jaya, Malaysia: Pelanduk Publications.

Dodge, Nicholas N.
  1981   The Malay-Aborigine Nexus under Malay Rule. Bijdragen
          Tot de Taal-, Land- en Volkenkunde van Nederlandsch-In-
          die 137(1):1-16.

Drakakis-Smith, David
  1992   Pacific Asia. London and New York: Routledge.

Dunn, F. L.
  1975   Rain-Forest Collectors and Traders: A Study of Resource
          Utilization in Modern and Ancient Malaya. Kuala Lumpur:
          Monographs of the Malaysian Branch of the Royal Asiatic
          Society, No. 5.

Edwin, Joseph
  1994a   Better Ways Sought to Help the Orang Asli. New Straits
          Times. June 2.
  1994b   Outdated Provisions in Act 'Must Be Amended.' New
          Straits Times. June 2.

Endicott, Karen
  1979   Batek Negrito Sex Roles. Unpublished Masters thesis, The
          Australian National University.

Endicott, Kirk
  1979a   Batek Negrito Religion: The World-view and Rituals of a
          Hunting and Gathering People of Peninsular Malaysia. Ox-
          ford: Clarendon Press.
  1979b   The Impact of Economic Modernization on the Orang Asli
          (Aborigines) of Northern Peninsular Malaysia. In Issues in
          Malaysian Development. J. C. Jackson and M. Rudner, eds.
          Pp. 167-204. Singapore: Heinemann Educational Books
          (Asia) Ltd.
  1982   The Effects of Logging on the Batek of Malaysia. Cultural
          Survival Quarterly 6(2):19-20.
  1983   The Effects of Slave Raiding on the Aborigines of the Malay
          Peninsula. In Slavery, Bondage and Dependency in South-
          east Asia. A. Reid, ed. Pp. 216-245. Brisbane: University of
          Queensland Press.
  1984   The Economy of the Batek of Malaysia: Annual and Histor-
          ical Perspectives. Research in Economic Anthropology 6:29-
          52.
  1987   The Effects of Government Policies and Programs on the Or-
          ang Asli of Malaysia. In Southeast Asian Tribal Groups and
          Ethnic Minorities in the 1980s. Jason Clay, ed. Pp. 47-51. Oc-
          casional Paper #22. Cambridge, Mass.: Cultural Survival,
          Inc.

Fanon, Frantz
  1968 [1961] The Wretched of the Earth. New York: Grove Press.

Farush Khan
  1982a   Logging Land Wrangle. New Straits Times. October 18.
  1982b   Orang Asli: We Were Conned Before. New Straits Times.
           October 20.
Favre, P.
  1848   An Account of the Wild Tribes Inhabiting the Malayan Pen-
           insula, Sumatra and a Few Neighboring Islands. Journal of
           the Indian Archipelago and Eastern Asia 2(1):237-282.
Fix, Alan G.
  1977   The Demography of the Semai Senoi. Anthropological Pa-
           pers of the Museum of Anthropology, University of Michi-
           gan, No. 62. Ann Arbor: Museum of Anthropology,
           University of Michigan.
Gianno, Rosemary
  1990   Semelai Culture and Resin Technology. New Haven: The
           Connecticut Academy of Arts and Sciences.
Gomes, Alberto G.
  1982   Ecological Adaptation and Population Change: Semang
           Foragers and Temuan Horticulturists in West Malaysia. Re-
           search Report No. 12. Honolulu: East-West Environment
           and Policy Institute.
  1986   Looking-for-Money: Simple Commodity Production in the
           Economy of the Tapah Semai of Malaysia. Unpublished
           Ph.D. diss., The Australian National University.
  1987   Dependence on the Govt Will Hurt Orang Asli. The Star.
           July 22.
  1989   Things Are Not What They Seem: Semai Economy in the
           1980s. Akademika 35:47-54.
  1990   Confrontation and Continuity: Simple Commodity Produc-
           tion among the Orang Asli. *In* Tribal Peoples and Develop-
           ment in Southeast Asia. Lim Teck Ghee and A. G. Gomes,
           eds. Pp. 12-36. Kuala Lumpur: Department of Anthropology
           and Sociology, University of Malaya.
  1991   Commodification and Social Relations among the Semai of
           Malaysia. *In* Cash, Commoditisation and Changing Forag-
           ers. N. Peterson and Toshio Matsuyama, eds. Pp. 163-197.
           Senri Ethnological Studies No. 30. Osaka: National Museum
           of Ethnology.
Gouldsbury, Pamela
  1960   Jungle Nurse. London: Jarrolds Publishers Ltd.
Harjit Singh
  1983   500 Fail to Get Monthly Subsidy. New Straits Times. January
           15.

Hasan Mat Nor
   1989   Pengumpulan Semula Orang Asli di Betau: Satu Penelitan
             Rengkas. Academika 35:97-112.
   1993   Learning from the Gentle People. Sunday Star. December
             19.

Heidhues, M. F. S.
   1974   Southeast Asia's Chinese Minorities. Camberwell, Austra-
             lia: Longman.

Hind, Robert J.
   1984   The Internal Colonial Concept. Comparative Studies in So-
             ciety and History 26:543-568.

Holman, Dennis
   1958   Noone of the Ulu. London: Heinemann.

Hood Salleh
   1984   Orang Asli Perceptions of the Malay World: A Historical
             Perspective. Ilmu Masyarakat 6:68-76.
   1990   Orang Asli of Malaysia: An Overview of Recent Develop-
             ment Policy and Its Impact. *In* Tribal Peoples and Develop-
             ment in Southeast Asia. Lim Teck Ghee and A. G. Gomes,
             eds. Pp. 141-149. Kuala Lumpur: Department of Anthropol-
             ogy and Sociology, Universiti Malaya.

Hood Salleh and Hasan Mat Nor
   1984   Roads Are for Development? Some Aspects of Jah Het Social
             Change. Development Forum 14:19-27.

Hood Salleh and Ruth Kiew
   1990   The Role of Rattan in the Economy of Orang Asli Communi-
             ties: A Preliminary Field Report. Paper presented at the Sim-
             posium Ketiga: Mengenai Kehidupan Sosial dan
             Pembangunan Masyarakat Orang Asli di Semenanjung Ma-
             laysia, Bangi, Universiti Kebangsaan Malaysia, January 20.

Hooker, M. B.
   1967   Semai House Construction in Ulu Slim, Perak. Federation
             Museums Journal 12 (New Series):27-34.
   1976   The Personal Laws of Malaysia. Kuala Lumpur: Oxford Uni-
             versity Press.
   1991   The Orang Asli and the Laws of Malaysia with Special Ref-
             erence to Land. Ilmu Masyarakat 18:51-79.

Howell, Signe
   1995   The Indigenous People of Peninsular Malaysia: It's Now or
             Too Late. *In* Indigenous Peoples of Asia. R. H. Barnes, A.
             Gray, and B. Kingsbury, eds. Pp. 273-287. Monograph and
             Occasional Paper Series No. 48. Ann Arbor, Mich.: Associa-
             tion for Asian Studies, Inc.

Human Rights Watch and Natural Resources Defense Council
1992   Defending the Earth: Abuses of Human Rights and the Environment. New York: Human Rights Watch and Natural Resources Defense Council.

Hurst, Philip
1990   Rainforest Politics: Ecological Destruction in South-East Asia. London and New Jersey: Zed Books.

Hussein Mat Omar, C. Sivashanmugam, and Halimaton Ibrahim
1991   Perjuangan Kaum Asli untuk Tanah. Utusan Pengguna. December.

Ibrahim, S., and P. H. Chong
1992   Floristic Composition of Virgin Jungle Reserve (VJR) at Kuala Langat South Peat Swamp Forest, Selangor, Peninsular Malaysia. Malayan Nature Journal 46:85-95.

Ismail, Rose
1995   We Must Do More for the Orang Asli. New Sunday Times. June 25.

Jamal al-Din al-Afghani
1973 [1880-1881] Commentary on the Commentator. Nikki R. Keddie, trans. In The Islamic World. W. H. McNeill and M. Robinson, eds. Pp. 423-431. Chicago: University of Chicago Press.

Jesudason, James V.
1990   Ethnicity and the Economy: The State, Chinese Business, and Multinationals in Malaysia. Singapore: Oxford University Press.

Jeyakumar Devaraj
1993   Malnutrition Still a Problem. Pernloi Gah 5:11-12.

JHEOA
1983   Strategi Perkembangan Ugama Islam di Kalangan Masyarakat Orang Asli. Kuala Lumpur: Jabatan Hal Ehwal Orang Asli.

1989   Mesyuarat Mengenai Dakwah kepada Orang Asli Semenanjung Tanah Melayu. Kuala Lumpur: Jabatan Hal Ehwal Orang Asli.

Jimin B. Idris, Mohd Tap Salleh, Jailani M. Dom, Abd. Halim Haji Jawi, Md. Razim Shafie
1983   Planning and Administration of Development Programmes for Tribal Peoples (The Malaysian Setting). Kuala Lumpur: Jabatan Hal Ehwal Orang Asli.

Jones, Alun
1968   The Orang Asli: An Outline of Their Progress in Modern Malaya. Journal of Southeast Asian History 9(2):286-305.

Juhaidi Yean Abdullah
1995   Law Hinders Orang Asli Progress. New Sunday Times. May 28.

Juli Edo
1990   Tradisi Lisan Masyarakat Semai. Monograf Fakulti Sains Kemasyarakatan dan Kemanusiaan No. 16. Bangi, Malaysia: Universiti Kebangsaan Malaysia.
1991   Pendidikan. In Pembangunan Orang Asli dalam Konteks Wawasan 2020. Itam Wali et al., eds. Pp. 17-23. Kuala Lumpur: Jawatankuasa POASM dan Senator Orang Asli.

Karp, Jonathan
1994   Paper Chase. Far Eastern Economic Review. October 6:70-71.

Khor Geok Lin
1985   A Study of the Nutritional Status of the Semai. Unpublished Ph.D. diss., Universiti Malaya.

Lau, Leslie, and Loong Meng Yee
1995   No Evidence That Vogt Instigated Bateks, Says MB. The Star. June 8.

Leary, John D.
1995   Violence and the Dream People: The Orang Asli in the Malayan Emergency, 1948-1960. Monographs in International Studies, Southeast Asia Series, No. 95. Athens, Ohio: Center for International Studies, Ohio University.

Legal Correspondent
1991   Religious Rights and Freedom: The Law and the Orang Asli. Pernloi Gah 3:13-14.

Lim Hin Fui
1993   Integrating the Orang Asli (Malaysia's Aborigines) into the Main Stream of National Development: For Better or Worse? Paper presented at the XVth International Botanical Congress, Yokohama, August 28-September 3.

Little, Elbert L.
1980   The Audubon Society Field Guide to North American Trees. New York: Alfred A. Knopf.

LKW/C[olin] N[icholas]
1990   Bulldozed: Orang Asli Church in Selangor. Pernloi Gah 1:8-10.

Logan, J. R.
1847   The Superstitions of the Mintira, with Some Additional Remarks on their Customs, Etc. Journal of the Indian Archipelago and Eastern Asia 1:307-331.

Loh, Henry
1993   Leave Out the Cosmetics: Provide Sincere Development. Pernloi Gah 5:6-7.

Loong Meng Yee
1995   Vogt Appeals to Continue Batek Study. The Star. June 16.

Mabbett, Hugh, and Ping-Ching Mabbett
1972   The Chinese in Indonesia, The Philippines, and Malaysia. London: Minority Rights Group.

Mahathir bin Mohamad
1970   The Malay Dilemma. Singapore: Donald Moore for Asia Pacific Press.

Malay Mail
1984   Of 63,700 Orang Asli Living in 1,000 Villages. Malay Mail. July 23.

Malaysian Government
1982   Malaysia: Federal Constitution. Kuala Lumpur: Malaysian Government.
1994   Akta Orang Asli 1954 / Aboriginal Peoples Act 1954 (with all amendments up to June 1994). Kuala Lumpur: Malaysian Government.

Man Yuke Foong and Amelia Hoh
1987   Living in Fear of "Outsiders." Sunday Star. July 5.

Manavalan, Theresa
1985a   Hostel Neglect. Malay Mail. February 22.
1985b   Homes for Hostel. Malay Mail. February 23.
1985c   Garden School Plan. Malay Mail. June 25.

Matayun, Agatha
1993   Forced to Step Out into a Concrete Land. Sunday Star. November 28.

Maxwell, W. E.
1882   The History of Perak from Native Sources. Journal of the Straits Branch of the Royal Asiatic Society 9:85-108.

McClelland, D.
1962   The Achieving Society. Princeton: Van Nostrand.

McLellan, Susan
1983   Orang Asli: An Analysis of State Penetration and Development Plans on Aboriginal Peoples in West Malaysia. Unpublished paper presented at the XIth International Congress of Anthropological and Ethnological Sciences, Laval University, Quebec City, August 12-13.

Means, Gordon P.
1985-1986 The Orang Asli: Aboriginal Policies in Malaysia. Pacific Affairs 58:637-652.

Mills, C. Wright
1967   The Problem of Industrial Development. In Power, Politics and People: The Collected Essays of C. Wright Mills. Irving L. Horowitz, ed. Pp. 150-156. New York: Oxford University Press.

Milne, R. S., and D. K. Mauzy
  1986   Malaysia: Tradition, Modernity, and Islam. Boulder, Colo.,
            and London: Westview Press.

Ministry of Primary Industries
  1992   Forever Green: Malaysia and Sustainable Forest Manage-
            ment. Kuala Lumpur: Ministry of Primary Industries.

Ministry of the Interior
  1961   Statement of Policy Regarding the Administration of the
            Aborigine Peoples of the Federation of Malaya. Kuala Lum-
            pur: Ministry of the Interior.

Mitton, Roger
  1995   Power Play: Malaysia's Prime Minister is Facing a Strong
            Challenge from His Deputy. Asiaweek. October 20:24-28.

Mohd Tap bin Salleh
  1990   An Examination of Development Planning among the Rural
            Orang Asli of West Malaysia. Unpublished Ph.D. diss., Uni-
            versity of Bath.

Nagata, Judith
  1979   Malaysian Mosaic: Perspectives from a Poly-ethnic Society.
            Vancouver: University of British Columbia Press.

New Straits Times
  1982a   Call for Orang Asli MPs. New Straits Times. April 6.
  1982b   542 Orang Asli Families Regrouped. New Straits Times.
            May 18.
  1983   Religious Dept: No Force on Orang Asli. New Straits Times.
            August 15.
  1984   What Makes Orang Asli Low-achievers? New Straits Times.
            November 11.
  1988a   Negri to Continue Helping Orang Asli. New Straits Times.
            February 14.
  1988b   MB: Road Link Will Boost Perak's Growth. New Straits
            Times. March 10.
  1988c   Trengganu to Develop Areas Along New Highway. New
            Straits Times. March 10.
  1988d   Missionary Work for Jobless Grads. New Straits Times. No-
            vember 28.
  1988e   26 Thai Women, Two Locals Held. New Straits Times. Feb-
            ruary 22.
  1990   Orang Asli Act To Be Reviewed, Says Wan Sidek. New
            Straits Times. February 21.

New Sunday Times
  1983   Erasing the Prejudice. New Sunday Times. January 16.
  1986   A Better Life for the Orang Asli. New Sunday Times. No-
            vember 2.
  1995   Orang Asli Stereotyped. New Sunday Times. May 14.

Newbold, T. J.
1839   Political and Statistical Account of the British Settlements in the Straits of Malacca, vol. 2. London: John Murray.

Nicholas, Colin
1990   In the Name of the Semai? The State and Semai Society in Peninsular Malaysia. *In* Tribal Peoples and Development in Southeast Asia. Lim Teck Ghee and A. G. Gomes, eds. Pp. 68-88. Kuala Lumpur: Department of Anthropology and Sociology, Universiti Malaya.

1991a   Orang Asli and Human Rights. Petaling Jaya, Malaysia: Center for Orang Asli Concerns.

1991b   Orang Asli and Society: Update on Current Issues. Pernloi Gah 3:1-4.

1991c   Even with Piped Water Orang Asli Will Be Losers. New Straits Times. February 1.

1991d   Orang Asli and Development: Chased Away for a Runway. Pernloi Gah 3:5-6.

1991e   Making Orang Asli Labourers Not the Way to Integration. Malay Mail. November 13.

1992a   Orang Asli Official-speak: The Double-speak You Can Be Sure Is All Hogwash. Pernloi Gah 4:10-13.

1992b   Orang Asli Affairs: Updates from the Media. Pernloi Gah 5:17-18.

1992c   Orang Asli Swiddeners: Scapegoats for Forest Destruction. Petaling Jaya, Malaysia: Center for Orang Asli Concerns.

1992d   Orang Asli in Sepang Are Not Squatters. New Straits Times. September 11.

1993   Three Killed in Fight with Jahais. Petaling Jaya, Malaysia: Center for Orang Asli Concerns.

1994   Pathway to Dependence: Commodity Relations and the Dissolution of Semai Society. Monash Papers on Southeast Asia No. 33. Clayton, Victoria, Australia: Centre of Southeast Asian Studies, Monash University.

NNP
1992   Ali Baba Is Out, Golf Baba Is In. Aliran Monthly 12(10):20.
1993a   Wasted Votes. Aliran Monthly 13(2):20.
1993b   Cakap Tak Serupa Bikin. Aliran Monthly 13(3):20-21.

Noone, H. D.
1936   Report on the Settlements and Welfare of the Ple-Temiar Senoi of the Perak-Kelantan Watershed. Journal of the Federated Malay States Museums 19(1):1-85.

Oh, Yvonne
1993   Alleviating the Lot of Our Orang Asli. Sunday Star. January 3.

Ong, Aihwa
1987   Spirits of Resistance and Capitalist Discipline: Factory
         Women in Malaysia. Albany, N.Y.: State University of New
         York Press.

Ong Hean Chooi
1986   Ecology, Resource Utilization and Ethnobiology of the Te-
         muan at Ulu Langat, Selangor. Unpublished Ph.D. diss.,
         Universiti Malaya.

Ong Hock Chuan
1984   White Dot the Reds Put In. The Star. August 19.

Ooi Jin-Bee
1963   Land, People and Economy in Malaya. London: Longmans,
         Green and Co. Ltd.

Pernloi Gah
1991   Blame Them for the Weather. Pernloi Gah 2:8-10.
1993   Seeing Double: 3 Views of Orang Asli Development. Pernloi
         Gah 5:4.

POASM
1991   Pembangunan Orang Asli dalam Konteks Wawasan 2020.
         Kuala Lumpur: Jawatankuasa Bekerja POASM / Senator
         Orang Asli.

Pratap Chatterjee
1993   Asians Fight Against Golf Course Invasion. Utusan Kon-
         sumer 278:10-11.

Purcell, Victor
1948   The Chinese in Malaya. London and New York: Oxford Uni-
         versity Press.

Rachagan, S. Sothi
1990   Constitutional and Statutory Provisions Governing the Or-
         ang Asli. In Tribal Peoples and Development in Southeast
         Asia. Lim Teck Ghee and A. G. Gomes, eds. Pp. 101-111.
         Kuala Lumpur: Department of Anthropology and Sociolo-
         gy, Universiti Malaya.

Rambo, A. Terry
1979   Primitive Man's Impact on the Genetic Resources of the Ma-
         layan Tropical Rain Forest. Malaysian Applied Biology
         8(1):59-65.
1985   Primitive Polluters: Semang Impact on the Malaysian Trop-
         ical Rain Forest Ecosystem. Ann Arbor: Museum of Anthro-
         pology, University of Michigan.

Ramsey, Bruce
1994   An American Editor in Asia. Liberty 7(5):39-42.

Rigg, Jonathan
1991   Southeast Asia: A Region in Transition. London: Unwin Hy-
         man.

Robarchek, Clayton A.
1977   Semai Nonviolence: A Systems Approach to Understand-
        ing. Unpublished Ph.D. diss., University of California at
        Riverside.
1979   Conflict, Emotion, and Abreaction: Resolution of Conflict
        among the Semai Senoi. Ethos 7(2):104-123.

Roff, William R.
1967   The Origins of Malay Nationalism. New Haven: Yale Uni-
        versity Press.

Rohini Talalla
1984   Ethnodevelopment and the Orang Asli of Malaysia: A Case
        Study of the Betau Settlement for Semai-Senoi. Antipode: A
        Radical Journal of Geography 16(2):27-32.

Rose, Diana
1993   Forced to Rely on Frogs for Survival. Sunday Star. Decem-
        ber 19.

Rostow, W.
1960   The Stages of Economic Growth. Cambridge: Cambridge
        University Press.

Saiful Mahadhir Nordin
1991   Ruined Lives . . . and Graves. New Straits Times. November
        30.

Samir Amin
1991   Pertumbuhan Bukan Pembangunan. Ilmu Masyarakat
        20:44-50.

Schebesta, Paul
1928   Among the Forest Dwarfs of Malaya. London: Hutchinson
        and Co., Ltd.

Selva, T.
1991   Side-stepped by Development. Pernloi Gah 3:8-9.

Shaila Koshy
1993   Will They Ever Own Land? Sunday Star. December 19.

Siddique, Sharon, and Leo Suryadinata
1981-1982 Bumiputra and Pribumi: Economic Nationalism (Indig-
        inism) in Malaysia and Indonesia. Pacific Affairs 54(4):662-
        687.

Singh, Gurmit
1981   Destroying Malaysian Forests. In Where Have All the Flow-
        ers Gone: Deforestation in the Third World. Vinson H. Sut-
        live, ed. Studies in Third World Societies 13:181-190.

Solheim, Wilhelm G., II
1980   Searching for the Origins of the Orang Asli. Federation Mu-
        seums Journal 25 (New Series):61-75.

Stewart, Kilton
1948   Magico-religious Beliefs and Practises in Primitive Society: A Sociological Interpretation of Their Therapeutic Aspects. Unpublished Ph.D. diss., London School of Economics and Political Science, University of London.
1972 [1951] Dream Theory in Malaya. *In* Altered States of Consciousness. C. T. Tart, ed. Pp. 161-170. Garden City, N.Y.: Anchor.

Sturrock, A. J., and R. O. Winstedt, eds.
1957   Hikayat Awang Sulong Merah Muda. Malay Literature Series No. 5. Singapore: Malaya Publishing House.

Sullivan, Patrick
1982   Social Relations of Dependence in a Malay State: Nineteenth Century Perak. Monograph No. 10. Kuala Lumpur: Malaysian Branch of the Royal Asiatic Society.

Sunday Star
1993   From Deep Forests to the Banks of the Betau. Sunday Star. December 19.

Syed Azhar and Leslie Lau
1995   Keeping Tabs on Taman Negara's "Manser." The Star. June 2.

Tan Chee-Beng
1987   Ethnic Dimensions in the Constitution. *In* Reflections on the Malaysian Constitution. Tan Chee-Beng, ed. Pp. 245-264. Penang: Aliran Kesedaran Negara.

Tan Chee Khoon
1980   Shoddy Deal for the Orang Asli. The Star. November 26.

Tan, J.
1993   A Temuan Odyssey Continues: Sepang Folk Forced to Give Up Own Development for Others. Pernloi Gah 5:8-10.

The Star
1982   Orang Asli Need More Protection. The Star. November 23.
1992a   Yassin: Status Quo of Orang Asli Land Stays. The Star. June 27.
1992b   MB: Price for New Airport Land Is Fair. The Star. September 7.
1993   Mumbo Jumbo Stuff "Setback for Natives." The Star. December 2.
1995a   Vogt "Will Be Monitored." The Star. June 17.
1995b   Govt to Do More for Orang Asli Community. The Star. June 23.

Todd, Halinah
1985   Orang Asli Caged in by JOA Policies. New Straits Times. January 13.
1990   Stolen Birthright: Orang Asli Rapidly Losing Land. Utusan Konsumer 206:9-12.

Tweedie, M. W. F.
1953   The Stone Age in Malaya. Journal of the Malayan Branch of the Royal Asiatic Society 26(2):1-90.

Utusan Konsumer
1991   "No Golf Course" Gimmick. Utusan Konsumer 243:6.
1992a   Redang Land Deal Controversy: Shareholders Question $35m Acquisition at Berjaya EGM. Utusan Konsumer 258:9.
1992b   No Time for EIAs! Utusan Konsumer 258:20.
1992c   Timber Tales. Utusan Konsumer 296:6.
1992d   Of Useless Land and Uninformed Officials. Utusan Konsumer. December:7.
1992e   Project Should Have an EIA. Utusan Konsumer. December:7.
1992f   Goofing Over Golf Courses. Utusan Konsumer 258:4.
1993a   Public Pays a Heavy Price for Berjaya's Destructive Project. Utusan Konsumer 278:4.
1993b   Gambling with Golf Courses. Utusan Konsumer 278:1, 2.
1993c   Cheap Excuse. Utusan Konsumer 278:3.
1993d   Understanding "Economic Jargon" in the Budget. Utusan Konsumer 288:9.
1994a   CAP: Revamp Laws on Hill Protection. Utusan Konsumer 294:6.
1994b   Harmful Highland Projects in M'sia. Utusan Konsumer 294:10-11.

Vogt, Christian
1995   A Friend of the Batek. Aliran Monthly 15(8):30-33.

Williams-Hunt, P. D. R.
1952   An Introduction to the Malayan Aborigines. Kuala Lumpur: The Government Press.

Williams-Hunt, Bah Tony
1991   Victims of Urbanization: The Temuans of Bukit Lanjan. Pernloi Gah 3:12.
1992   Contemporary Needs and Aspirations: Orang Asli Memorandum to the Government. Pernloi Gah 4:5-6.